Penguin Education

Penguin Modern Economics Texts
General Editor: B. J. McCormick

Political Economy
Editor: K. J. W. Alexander

Elements of Regional Economics
Harry W. Richardson

Harry W. Richardson

Elements of Regional Economics

Penguin Education

Penguin Education
A Division of Penguin Books Ltd,
Harmondsworth, Middlesex, England
Penguin Books Inc, 7110 Ambassador Road,
Baltimore, Md 21207, U.S.A.
Penguin Books Australia Ltd, Ringwood,
Victoria, Australia
Penguin Books Canada Ltd,
41 Steelcase Road West,
Markham, Ontario, Canada

First published 1969
Reprinted 1970, 1973
Copyright © Harry W. Richardson, 1969

Made and printed in Great Britain by
C. Nicholls & Company Ltd
Set in Monotype Times

Penguin Modern Economics Texts

This volume is one in a series of unit texts designed to reduce the price of knowledge for students of economics in universities and colleges of higher education. The units may be used singly or in combination with other units to form attractive and unusual teaching programmes. The volumes will cover the major teaching areas but they will differ from conventional books in their attempt to chart and explore new directions in economic thinking. The traditional divisions of theory and applied, of positive and normative and of micro and macro will tend to be blurred as authors impose new and arresting ideas on the traditional corpus of economics. Some units will fall into conventional patterns of thought but many will transgress established beliefs.

Penguin Modern Economics Texts are published in units in order to achieve certain objectives. First, a large range of short texts at inexpensive prices gives the teacher flexibility in planning his course and recommending texts for it. Secondly, the pace at which important new work is published requires the project to be adaptable. Our plan allows a unit to be revised or a fresh unit to be added with maximum speed and minimal cost to the reader.

The international range of authorship will, it is hoped, bring out the richness and diversity in economic analysis and thinking.

B.J.MCC.

Contents

Editorial Foreword 9

Preface 11

Introduction: Why Regional Economics? 13

Part One **The Homogeneous Region (Inter-regional Macroeconomics)** 17

1 Regional Income 19

2 Regional Growth 45

Part Two **The Nodal Region** 67

3 Location and Agglomeration 70

4 The Nodal Hierarchy 88

Part Three **The Planning Region** 109

5 Problems in Regional Planning 111

6 The Direction of Regional Policy 120

7 Some Regional Planning Techniques 139

Conclusion 151

References 153

Index 161

Editorial Foreword

In Britain, it is probably fair to say, regional policy has moved too far ahead of 'regional science' for all of its components to be sound and consistent with its objectives, whereas in the United States the comparable gap has been between a lagging regional policy and a rapidly advancing 'regional science'. Regional economics is only a part of 'regional science', just as regional economic policy can only be a part of regional policy. Wide gaps have existed between the approaches of economists, geographers, demographers and 'physical planners'. Only in recent years have these gaps been narrowing rapidly enough for us justifiably to expect very much more refinement from regional policy-makers than we have had so far.

This book is a remarkably compact introduction to regional economics. In addition it integrates economics with the other components of 'regional science', and makes an important contribution of its own to closing the gaps referred to above. The emphasis placed upon space and distance will be helpful to those economists who abstract from these important influences on economic decision-taking. The book operates at a frontier where economics must become inter-disciplinary if it is to produce meaningful and useful insights. As one would hope in this context, the author successfully integrates theory and application. He incorporates the results of some original research and most valuably examines regional growth models empirically. When the data are too thin for this empirical treatment he discusses what would be required for testing to take place, an approach which will be helpful both to students and to research workers.

Inevitably the wide scope of the book has led the author to compress his argument in places. The reader is provided with an extensive list of references that enable him to fill in any gaps.

K.J.W.A.

Preface

Regional economics is a relatively new, rapidly developing branch of economics which has excited an increasingly large amount of interest in recent years. The volume of specialist periodical literature is mounting at a fast rate, yet it remains a subject marked by a dearth of textbooks. It is not an easy field to survey in such a short book. I have had to be selective, sometimes ruthlessly, in the topics I could discuss.

As an aid to digesting and arranging the material I found it necessary to impose a rather formal structure on the book by dividing it into three parts, according to the familiar classification of regions into homogeneous, nodal and planning regions. This separates conveniently for analysis inter-regional macro-economics, spatial and locational aspects, and policy and planning problems. Whereas Part One deals primarily with inter-regional relationships and abstracts from space, Part Two explicitly considers the role of location and distance and explores the spatial distribution of population and economic activity, particularly within regions. I hope my view that regional policy and planning must combine both *inter*-regional and *intra*regional analysis will be clear to the reader before he reaches the end of Part Three. Thus, the three parts of the book are merely an organizational aid and must not be taken to imply a division in the subject matter itself.

I wish to thank Professor Ken Alexander, Bill McConnachie, Peter Sloane and Joan Vipond for helpful comments, and Mrs Sally Maxwell and Miss Margaret Hay for efficient typing.

Introduction: Why Regional Economics?

This question is raised not because the subject needs any justification, but for the very opposite reason. The claims of regional economics are so obvious and clear-cut that what needs to be explained is why interest in it has developed so recently. There are several factors contributing to its retarded development.

One of the most important of these is the conservatism of the economics profession. Economists have been reluctant to accept that there is any regularity in the spatial organization of the economy. The neo-classicists were steeped in marginalism, and marginal analysis was frequently not applicable to the space dimension. They liked smooth curves which were amenable to calculus, while distance functions and other spatial parameters tend to exhibit inconvenient discontinuities. When they advanced beyond the static, spaceless world of their predecessors, they turned to dynamic problems convinced that time was the crucial dimension (and after all it did raise fascinating problems!). The analysis of distance and the spatial distribution of people and activities was felt to be the province of the geographers, a breed for whom economists have never had a high regard (quite unfairly, when we consider the advances in economic geography in the last decade or two). The few economists who delved into locational problems were obscure central Europeans with names difficult to pronounce, whereas the giants of the profession in the twentieth century have been either Anglo–American or have emigrated to and worked in one of these two countries. It is perhaps not surprising that the spatial distribution of activities was regarded as being determined primarily by non-economic factors, and that location was not considered an important economic variable. These attitudes had serious results for the development of economic analysis; for example, economists could confidently assume that international trade can be analysed in a zero transport cost world.

The slow growth of interest in regional economics cannot be explained solely in terms of stubbornness and blinkered thinking. If we adopt classical assumptions, such as price flexibility and perfect mobility of factors, then differences between regions in prices, costs and incomes cannot persist. Perfect competition and the stable equilibrium concept could, it was believed, be entrusted to ensure that any disturbance in regional balance would be corrected by market forces. The imperceptible changes within the regional system were very hard to detect at a time when regional statistics were so much more imperfect and incomplete than they are now, so that it was possible to subscribe to the 'equality doctrine' because the neo-classical predictions on which it is based were so difficult to test.

The development of regional economics as an academic discipline has been accelerated by its policy implications. Events of the last fifty years have made it increasingly clear that market forces do not *inevitably* result in regional income equalization. Factor movements may be disequilibrating, and lagging regions may suffer from capital flight as well as out-migration. Agglomeration economies may favour a further build-up in prosperous areas. But disillusion with the doctrine of non-intervention is not the only prerequisite for a regional policy. It was no use intervening to alter the distribution of industry if industries were location-bound. Twentieth-century technological change has freed a great deal of manufacturing industry from its previous dependence on raw material and energy locations. Even more important, an effective regional policy could only be implemented in a 'full employment' economy. It is not very sensible for a government to make a great deal of fuss about regional inequities in conditions of general unemployment, for aggregate full employment ranks much higher among government objectives. Similarly, the pressure for regional intervention is based primarily on equity grounds, and income distribution goals are likely to receive much attention only after employment goals have been satisfied. In any event, regional policy measures are probably ineffective in conditions below full employment; migrants move more easily in booms than in slumps, while firms are more likely to be persuaded to relocate when they are expanding.

In the post-war period, the attainment of full employment and the development of new techniques of economic analysis have facilitated the growth of regional economics as a separate and distinct branch of economics. The greatest stimulus of all has derived from the realization that regional economic analysis has direct policy implications, not only for location-of-industry measures but for regional and sub-regional planning. In addition, as economists have begun to inquire into new fields for investigation, it has been increasingly recognized that problems of location and space are worthy of analysis in their own right.

Part One The Homogeneous Region
(Inter-regional Macroeconomics)

The homogeneous region concept is based on the view that
geographical areas might be linked together as a single region when
they share uniform characteristics. These characteristics might be
economic (such as similar production structures or homogeneous
consumption patterns), geographical (such as a similar topography
or climate), even social or political (such as a regional 'identity'
or a traditional party allegiance). However, areas which are uniform
in some respects may be dissimilar in others, and attempts by geographers to delimit the boundaries of homogeneous regions
have all foundered on this difficulty.

For the economist a possible criterion for defining the homogeneous region is similarity in *per capita* income levels. A region
defined in these terms is essentially spaceless, because such a
definition implies that a region grows and declines as a whole
rather than total income changing as a result of separate influences
on economic activities located at different centres within a region.
The national economy can accordingly be treated as a set of
spatially separated points which we may call 'regions'. The
influence of distance and of spatial differences within regions is
ignored in such an analysis, and regions are merely regarded as
components of a multisector economy.

We may describe this approach to regional analysis as inter-
regional macroeconomics. This derives from a scaling down of
national income and growth models to the regional level, though
each region is also treated as an open economy so that the models
determine inter-regional trade and factor flows as well as regional
income. Key problems such as regional income change, fluctuations,
stabilization policy and the determinants of regional growth may be
analysed within such a framework.

Regional macroeconomics implicitly assumes homogeneity.
Why? It aims at predicting short- and long-run variations in
regional economic activity in terms of the interaction of certain
parametric variables (e.g. the marginal propensities to consume

and to import, the marginal capital–output ratio). These variables cannot be used successfully for prediction unless they have similar constant values *over the region as a whole* or unless they change in a regular, foreseeable way. These conditions would not hold if the over-all regional values were the average of very wide variations within different parts of the region. Thus, when we extend macroeconomic theory to regional analysis we abstract from differences within regions and treat each region as homogeneous and, ultimately, as spaceless.

1 Regricional Income

Export Base Theory

Export base theory provides the simplest form of regional income model. It cannot really be classified as a part of inter-regional macroeconomics because it reduces a regional system to the region under consideration and the rest of the world. Its importance lies in the fact that it supplies the theoretical framework for many empirical regional multiplier studies.

The central assumption of the theory is that exports are the *sole* autonomous item of expenditure. All other components of expenditure are treated as functions of income, and the expenditure and import functions are both assumed to have no intercepts but pass through the origin. Thus for Region i we may write:

$$Y_i = (E_i - M_i) + X_i \qquad \qquad 1$$
$$\text{income} = \underset{\text{spending}}{\text{domestic}} + \text{exports}$$

$$E_i = e_i Y_i \qquad \qquad 2$$
$$M_i = m_i Y_i \qquad \qquad 3$$
$$X_i = \bar{X}_i \text{ (exogenous).} \qquad \qquad 4$$

Substituting 2, 3 and 4 into 1 we obtain:

$$Y_i = e_i Y_i - m_i Y_i + \bar{X}_i.$$

Therefore
$$Y_i = \frac{\bar{X}_i}{1 - e_i + m_i}. \qquad \qquad 5$$

Regional income is therefore a multiple of exports provided that the marginal propensity to spend locally $(e - m)$ is less than unity.

Rearranging **5** we can see that

$$\frac{Y_i}{X_i} = \frac{1}{1 - e_i + m_i}.\qquad\qquad 6$$

Thus, if we measure the ratio of exports to total income then its reciprocal *is* the multiplier. Critics of base theory sometimes suggest that the ratio of total exports to aggregate income is used only as a proxy for the marginal ratio in multiplier estimation. But the theory and, in particular, its assumption of no exogenous elements other than exports make the average and marginal ratios equal. The base multiplier

$$K_i = \frac{1}{1 - e_i + m_i}$$

is the result if we differentiate income with respect to exports i.e. $dY_i/d\bar{X}_i$. Consequently, the assumptions of the model determine that

$$\frac{Y_i}{X_i} = \frac{dY_i}{d\bar{X}_i}.\qquad\qquad 7$$

An often quoted drawback of these models is that the size of the export base is an inverse function of the size of a region. It is sometimes implied that this is a crucial objection to base theory since we can more or less obtain any multiplier value we desire by varying the scale of the region studied. But multiplier values are in fact higher for large regions. A large region will tend to have a smaller export base but it will also have a low m, and this will tend to raise K; conversely a small area will have not only a high export–income ratio but also a high m both of which will tend to reduce K. Though the variation of the importance of the export base with scale of area remains awkward for the usefulness of base theory an offsetting factor is the covariation of $\bar{X}/Y$ and m.

An Inter-Regional Income Model

For a more satisfactory regional income model we need to alter the assumptions of the export base model. The crucial change is that exports are no longer treated as the sole autonomous expenditure component. Firstly, we make allowance for autonomous consumption and for investment and government spending both of which are assumed to be determined exogenously. Secondly, by moving from the single region– 'rest-of-the-world' case to a true inter-regional system of n regions, we do not have to regard exports as autonomous at all. In a closed system, a region's exports will be determined by the import demands of other regions of the system. Finally, since we have introduced government spending, it is logical to include taxes in the model and to make private consumption spending a function of disposable income. Although the model, could take account of transfer payments, lump-sum taxes, direct and indirect taxes (falling on consumption and/or investment), I shall make the simplifying assumption that all taxes fall upon income.

Our improved regional income model can be represented as follows:

$$Y_i = C_i + I_i + G_i + X_i - M_i \qquad 8$$

where Y, C, I, G, X and M have their usual meanings;

$$C_i = a_i + c_i Y_i^d \qquad 9$$

where Y^d = disposable income and c = marginal propensity to consume;

$$I_i = \bar{I}_i \qquad 10$$

$$G_i = \bar{G}_i \qquad 11$$

$$X_i = \sum_{j=1} M_{ij} = \sum_{j=1} m_{ij} Y_j^d \qquad 12$$

$$M_i = \sum_{j=1} m_{ji} Y_i^d \qquad 13$$

$$Y_i^d = Y_i - T_i \qquad 14$$

$$T_i = t_i Y_i \qquad 15$$

where t = marginal rate of taxation.

$$A_i = a_i + \bar{I}_i + \bar{G}_i \qquad 16$$

where A_i = total autonomous expenditures.

Substituting equations 9–16 into 8, and rearranging yields the income equation

$$Y_i = \frac{A_i + \sum_{j=1} m_{ij} Y_j (1 - t_j)}{1 - (c_i - \sum_{j=1} m_{ji})(1 - t_i)}. \qquad 17$$

The income of Region i thus consists of the sum of autonomous expenditures plus exports × the multiplier

$$\frac{1}{1-(c_i- \sum_{j=1} m_{ji})(1-t_i)} \, . \, [1]$$

This model is very different from the export base model described earlier. A change in regional income can now follow from several possible sources, not merely from a change in exogenously determined exports as in export base theory. These sources include: (a) a variation in regional autonomous expenditures (e.g. investment, government spending); (b) a change in the income level of any other region (regions) in the system which will show itself in a change in Region i's exports; (c) a shift in any of the model's parameters (marginal propensity to consume, the inter-regional trade coefficients or the marginal rate of taxation).

This regional income model can also be used for analysis of regional stabilization policy. Since government spending is one of the autonomous expenditure variables, we may use the model to explore the effects of changes in the over-all level of government expenditure and/or its regional distribution. We can refine the model to take account of more sophisticated tax structures, and we may link the level of government spending to total tax revenues (Airov, 1967; Engerman, 1965; Peacock, 1965).

The conditions of stability for the system and the repercussions of changes in the regional distribution of autonomous expenditures are particularly important in the context of stabilization policy. If the marginal propensities to consume in all regions are less than unity, then the system is stable. If, on the other hand, either all marginal propensities to consume

1. An alternative multiplier is obtained if we drop the assumption of all investment being determined exogenously and allow for induced investment. If we assume that the induced investment $I_i^{ind} = v_i Y_i$, where v_i = marginal propensity to investment then the multiplier becomes

$$\frac{1}{1-(c_i- \sum_{j=1} m_{ji})(1-t_i)-v_i} \, .$$

exceed unity or regions with such high propensities predominate, then the system is unstable. Whether the marginal propensities to consume are equal or unequal is also of some consequence.

Chipman (1950, p. 122) showed that if $c_i = c_j$ for all regions $(i, j, \ldots, n)$ then the inter-regional multiplier reduces to the simple national multiplier formula. This means that with equal marginal propensities to consume, changes in the regional allocation of government spending (or other autonomous expenditures) will not change the level of national income but will only affect regional income levels. Where $c_i \neq c_j$, however, changes in the geographical distribution of expenditures will result in changes in the level of national income. Assuming no regional capacity constraints, the increase in national income will be maximized if the increase in government expenditure is concentrated in the regions with the highest c (usually the most underdeveloped regions).

It is important to note that where the objective is to maximize national income, the optimal distribution of expenditure is independent of the values of the inter-regional trade coefficients. With more complex objectives, such as a prescribed distribution of income changes over several (or all) regions, the marginal propensity to import values becomes relevant (Engerman, 1965).

The virtue of an inter-regional income model of this type is that it explains why it may be necessary to cut government spending in some regions in order to raise income levels in all regions. In particular, reference to such a model may help to make regional and national interests compatible by demonstrating to the residents of a given region that a cut in their share of government spending in the interests of efficiency may be offset by export expansion as a result of increases in government spending in other regions.

Income spillovers and the possibility of secondary export repercussions are the most distinctive features of inter-regional income models. An investment injection in Region i will not only raise income (a rise in A_i) in that region, but the stimulus will spread to all other regions of the system[1] via an increase in M_i ($= \sum\limits_{j=1} M_{ji}$). If the initial situation is one of balance-of-payments equilibrium the induced rise in imports will mean a deterioration in Region i's balance of payments. This is not, however, the final net effect. Income expansion in other regions will boost Region i's exports – exports will in fact rise by

$$\sum_{j=1} m_{ij} \frac{\Delta Y_j}{\Delta A_i} (1-t_j).$$

The over-all effect on Region i's balance of payments depends on how far the primary change (induced imports) is offset by the secondary change (the rise in exports.) In most conceivable situations the secondary rise in exports will not be large enough to prevent a deterioration in the balance of payments of Region i.

For an improvement in Region i's balance of payments we need the coincidence of marginal propensities to consume greater than unity in several other regions of the system (in fact, marginal propensities to consume greater than one must preponderate when weighted by their respective marginal propensities to import). The condition for balance-of-payments improvement is that the inter-regional multiplier for Region i must be greater than the closed economy multiplier

$$\frac{1}{1-c_i(1-t_i)}.$$

Regions may suffer from balance-of-payments problems, though because of data deficiencies these are much less publicized than in the international economy. It is commonly assumed that the balance-of-payments adjustment mechanism operates more effectively between regions than between nations. Certainly, there are marked differences in the two institutional frameworks (i.e. the inter-regional economy and the international economy). Regions cannot avail themselves of the policy instruments (exchange rate, tariff, monetary and fiscal measures) open to nations. Moreover, remedying a

1. This assumes the indecomposable case where each region trades directly or indirectly with every other region.

balance-of-payments deficit is unlikely to figure prominently, if at all, among a region's policy objectives, though both regional policy-makers and the national government may intervene to deal with weaknesses (such as high unemployment rates or high net migration) which might be the by-product of persistent balance-of-payments problems. Another difference between a national and international economy is that factors have in general a higher degree of mobility between regions, and that factor flows may have an equilibrating function in the regional balance of payments.

Balance-of-payments equilibrium in each region is not an essential requirement for income and employment equilibrium. In an open system, it is only necessary for a region's balance of payments to be in equilibrium with other regions and foreign countries considered together. If this condition holds for all regions, then balance-of-payments equilibrium is also attained in the national economy. Moreover, an import surplus can be maintained if combined with an excess of domestic investment over savings. Thus, income equilibrium in a region is compatible with a current account deficit if the import surplus is financed by an inflow of savings from outside the region.

Temporary disequilibrium in a region's balance of payments may be remedied by movements of short-term funds (i.e. by inter-regional transfers between the branches of banks). In many cases, however, additional mechanisms of adjustment may be required. These include price and income effects, government transfers and government spending in depressed regions, and flows of capital and labour. Price effects are unlikely to be very effective; wages will be sticky – especially downwards – though some flexibility may result from regional variations in 'earnings drift'; price adjustments will be limited because the majority of producers will cater for national rather than regional markets, and the prices they fix will tend to rule everywhere. Income effects, too, may be insufficient to restore equilibrium, but they may be more effective than in the international economy, because m is usually larger for regions than for the nation. Fiscal operations may also assist the equilibrating process either by built-in stabilizers or by direct government spending in depressed regions. Although an inflow of government funds will itself increase imports, it will nevertheless make some contribution to reducing the balance-of-payments deficit provided that $c + m < 1$ (de Scitovsky, 1958, pp. 80–95).

The above mechanisms of adjustment assume that the origin of a balance-of-payments deficit is an export decline. If, on the other hand, a region runs into deficit as a result of income expansion as in our inter-regional income model, then these mechanisms will tend to disequilibrate. The distinction between these two sources of balance-of-payments deficit is crucial when we consider the role of factor flows. Capital will tend to move to high yield regions, but this will equilibrate only if the relevant model is that where the deficit is caused by a process of income expansion; in other words, if prosperous regions run the import surpluses.

Chronic balance-of-payments problems are more likely to arise in a region as a consequence of export decline, and in such a case capital will tend to flow out rather than in. The converse holds in regard to labour migration. If labour moves at all it will migrate to high-income regions. Where the deficit develops according to our model, it will therefore move in the wrong direction. But if the balance-of-payments deficit is due to structural disequilibrium (e.g. a fall in exports) migrants may move from depressed to prosperous regions, and their earnings in the latter will add to regional income and to import demand.

Whatever the source of balance-of-payments deficit, therefore, capital and labour will tend to move in the same direction, but these flows will offset each other as a means of balance-of-payments adjustment. Factor flows are not, however, important mechanisms of adjustment for the short-run balance-of-payments disturbances of the kind predicted by our inter-regional income model. They are more important as forces of adjustment to the regional growth process, though even in the long run they may widen rather than narrow regional growth rates.

Applications of the Economic Base

Despite the weaknesses of base theory, there have been many attempts to carry out empirical studies to separate the basic from the non-basic sectors of a region (or a city – in fact, most studies, for example Pfouts (1960) and Tiebout (1962), have referred to the urban base). Such exercises can be worthwhile provided we recognize their limitations, and use the results merely to throw some light on the region's structure rather than as a tool for short-run or long-run projections.

Base analysis is really concerned with the identification of basic *income*, but the scarcity of regional income data (especially in the U.K.) necessitates the use of proxy indicators, usually employment or, in rare cases, sales, value added or wage bills. Discontinuities in employment make it a fairly insensitive indicator of changes in base activity. Regional income will rise immediately in response to base expansion, but employment will rise only in the long run (theoretically, this difficulty can be solved by assuming no excess capacity and that employment is a linear and stable function of income). Employment data also suffer from their inability to take account of the differential effects of base expansion on income according to the relative wage levels of the industries affected, and similarly ignore the long-run effects of increases in productivity from industry to industry. More seriously, a high proportion of a region's income payments may be unearned income, and the influence of unearned income on a region's base ratio obviously cannot be reflected in measures of employment.

Several methods have been adopted to divide regions into basic and non-basic categories. The most straightforward, but also the most expensive and the most time-consuming, is to measure the base directly by use of standard survey and questionnaire methods. Although this approach may often avoid the use of employment as the indicator, the surveys necessary may be voluminous, requiring not merely questionnaires to industrial and financial establishments, but also shopping surveys and other means of obtaining information

about the source of custom, when this is not identifiable by
the establishment itself. Not only are the results dependent
upon high response rates, but the method is not without conceptual difficulties such as to how to deal with sectors not
producing marketable goods and services, and the dangers
of misallocation of output (into local use rather than
indirect exports) arising from complex input–output connexions.

It is more usual to employ indirect methods which fall into
two types – the *ad hoc* assumption approach and the location
quotient (L.Q.) method and its variants. The first of these
arbitrarily assigns sectors either to the export category (such
as manufacture and agriculture) or to the local, non-basic
group (distribution, local government, banking and finance,
entertainment, etc.). Sometimes, this is slightly refined by
leaving a (possibly large) group of 'mixed' sectors and estimating the base component of these by other means. The errors
of the assumption approach can be very large. Many manufacturing establishments, for example in building materials,
printing and food processing, may cater for local needs, and
the local market orientation of the manufacturing sector will
tend to increase with the size of the region. Some service
establishments (head offices of building societies or insurance
companies and research and development centres are two
obvious examples) are clearly non-local. Even service sectors
with a very low drawing radius such as shops, cinemas or
doctors in general practice cannot be wholly placed in the
non-basic category in a region which benefits from substantial
tourist activity.

Moreover, the products of social service establishments and
government activities which are not sold on the market, and
which may cater for local needs, cannot be placed in the non-
basic sector on an *ad hoc* basis. Basic sectors are not export
sectors alone in the narrow sense, but include all activities
which are not closely tied to the level of economic activity
inside the region. In other words, they encompass all activities
which are sustained externally including those which are
maintained by external financial support, especially that of the

government. In dividing a school, university, hospital, public works programme, etc. into basic and non-basic components, we need to be able to determine how much of its financial support derives from the region and how much from outside.

The L.Q. technique is the one most commonly adopted in empirical base studies. We work out the L.Q.s for each individual industry in the region (using the nation as a whole as the reference norm), and use quotients greater than unity to indicate the presence of export activity. This assumes that if a region is more specialized than the nation in the production of a particular good, then it exports that good according to how specialized it is. In other words, we assume that local specialization in production implies local export of surplus production.

The size of the base is most easily estimated by calculating, for each sector with its L.Q. > 1, an *index of surplus workers*, (i.e. the difference between actual regional industry employment and the region's *pro rata* share of national industry employment), and then repeating the process for each industry summing all the surplus workers to yield an estimate of base employment[1] (Matilla and Thompson 1955). The rest of the region's labour force is assigned to the non-basic category.

The underlying assumptions of the L.Q. method seriously weaken its reliability. It assumes that the pattern of demand in each region is identical to that of the nation, that productivity per worker in each regional sector is the same as in national industries, and that the nation is a closed economy.[2] These assumptions will not hold in most cases, and although allowance can be made for this the procedures become much more complicated. Another difficulty is that the level of exports

1. Thus, if an industry within a region requires 25,000 workers to have a location quotient equal to unity but, in fact, has a labour force of 33,000 then we assume that the extra 8,000 serve export markets.

2. If the L.Q. $= 1$, this implies that the region supplies its own needs only if the nation supplies its own needs. If some national industries export, then this method understates the base by neglecting exports to other *countries*.

depends on the level of disaggregation. If we keep to broad aggregates, imports and exports concealed in finer sub-categories may cancel each other out, so that the base estimate developed from the larger categories seriously understates the size of the base. The more we disaggregate, the more reliable the technique becomes.

The drawbacks of the method should not be overstressed. It has two important advantages. Firstly, it takes care of indirect as well as direct exports. For instance, a steel plant may sell most of its output to a local car manufacturer ex-porting cars; this is locally sold but is tied indirectly to exports, and this fact will be revealed by the L.Q. approach. Secondly, the method is inexpensive and can be applied to historical data to reveal trends. Despite their deficiencies, L.Q. methods will yield an estimate, probably an underestimate, of base activity.

Some years ago, Ullman and Dacey (1960) suggested a modification of the above method, the *minimum requirements technique*, which they applied to urban base studies though it is equally applicable to regions on the condition that a large set is chosen. Within the large group, the procedure is to estimate the percentage of the labour force employed in each industry, and rank the percentages for a given industry in decreasing order. We presume that the smallest percentage is the minimum required by any region to satisfy its own needs, and therefore all employment in other regions above this percentage is considered as base employment; the process is then repeated for all industries to yield the over-all base estimate. A refine-ment is to accept that a few regional structures may be so odd and atypical that it is safer to exclude a number (or a given percentile) from the bottom rank and use the lowest remaining figure as a bench-mark. But how do we select the cut-off point, in view of the fact that the higher this point the less each region will export? Moreover, low rank regions may hold their position in a sector not because they supply their own needs, but because they import their requirements on a large scale.

The suggestion that the minimum requirements approach is an advance on the traditional L.Q. method has recently been criticized by Pratt (1968). He shows that the theoretical implication of the technique is the paradoxical one where all regions export but none imports, and argues that the identical demand and productivity assumptions of the L.Q. approach are also necessary to the newer method. Moreover, he points out that there is no objective reason why minima should make a better basis for reference than the averages which form the basis of the L.Q. treatment. Finally, disaggregation into smaller sectors actually reduces the reliability of the minimum requirements technique whereas it improves the accuracy of the L.Q. method. This is because with exceedingly fine disaggregation the minimum requirements for most categories would be near zero, suggesting that regions have virtually no internal needs and that most production goes for export. Manipulation of the level of disaggregation can yield almost any results we would like to confirm. More constructively, Pratt argues that if the minimum requirements technique has any value its converse, a maximum requirements approach, can be used. Now we assume that the area with the maximum percentage employment in each sector meets exactly its own internal needs. This implies a model in which no region exports just as the opposite approach implies no imports. If the two methods were used together, however, the parameters may be adjustable in a way which makes imports and exports balance.

Regional Multiplier Estimates

Most early attempts to estimate regional employment multipliers relied on the export base approach. Export base studies have many valuable uses, but they do not give us a predictive multiplier.

I have carried out an export base exercise for North-East Scotland[1], which illustrates the gross unreliability of base multiplier estimates compared with plausible values for the regional multiplier. Using D.E.P. data, location quotients were estimated for employment in each industry by minimum

1. Defined as the counties of Aberdeenshire, Banffshire, Kincardineshire, Moray and Nairn.

list heading for June 1966 in North-East Scotland using Great Britain as a bench-mark.[1] The L.Q. estimates were cross-checked for manufacturing sectors against geographical distribution of sales estimates obtained from direct survey methods.[2] Numbers of surplus workers in industries with L.Q.s above unity were calculated; aggregated together these yielded an estimate of total base employment. Additions to the base had to be made to take account of defence[3] bases in the area not included in D.E.P. statistics and to make allowance for overseas exporting activity ignored by the L.Q. technique which assumes a closed national economy. The result was a base–service ratio of 1:1·3 or a base multiplier of 2·3 This is much higher than plausible estimates of the regional multiplier for this area. It is of course an average ratio whereas a marginal ratio is required; even if we assume linear functions and constant coefficients $dY/dX \neq Y/X$ when there is any autonomous expenditure component other than exports.

The marginal ratio may fluctuate widely. The repercussions on local income and employment will vary according to the sector in which base expansion occurs. This suggests an improved reliability if we disaggregate the export base. This is the *differential multiplier* approach suggested by Weiss and Gooding (1968). The local repercussions vary because of (i) differences in spending habits of workers in separate export sectors and (ii) differences in the degree of local interindustry linkages. They identified three separate export sectors in Portsmouth, New Hampshire: a defence base, a government shipyard and private manufacturing. They found that the multiplier was smallest for the defence base and largest for

1. I am grateful to Mrs D. Hatvany for research assistance.
2. These were obtained from the Manufacturing Survey undertaken as part of the Aberdeen University inquiry into the Development Potential of North-East Scotland commissioned by the Scottish Development Department, 1966–8.
3. U.S. studies, however, suggest that the local multiplier effects of defence bases are considerably lower than those of private manufacturing. See, for example, Weiss and Gooding (1968).
4. The three employment multipliers were 1·4, 1·6 and 1·8 respectively.

private manufacturing.[4] The value of their model depends on the assumptions that the sectors are independent (i.e. inter-industry linkages between them are negligible) and that workers and firms in export sectors divide their local spending among service activities in a similar manner.

Another improvement in export base studies is to estimate the income rather than the employment multiplier. This is a much trickier task requiring field surveys, and is prohibitively expensive except for a small community. One study of a Chicago suburb was carried out some years ago by Tiebout (1960). His model was a simple one:

$$Y = Y_x + Y_n \qquad\qquad 18$$

total income = exogenous + endogenous income

$$Y_x = \overline{Y}_x \qquad\qquad 19$$

$$Y_n = a + bY. \qquad\qquad 20$$

Exports are included in Y_x while local sales, etc. are included in Y_n. Tiebout assumed $a = 0$, so that the endogenous income function passed through the origin with the result that the marginal is assumed equal to the average propensity to consume local goods. His estimate of b (the *income-creating* propensity to spend in Winnetka) was 0·0384 reflecting high leakages in a small suburb due to most secondary spending being made in Chicago itself.[1] The community income multiplier $(1/1-b)$ is consequently 1·04.

There are other methods of estimating regional multipliers.[2] Even intuition combined with a few rough and ready facts

1. In the first round of spending, the average propensity to consume local goods was 0·277 but every unit of local sales of goods and services only gave rise to 0·139 units of local income created.

2. I ignore in the following paragraphs the restrictive assumptions of the multiplier model which may detract from the usefulness of empirical verification. These include: the presence of unused resources to enable real output to expand, an elastic supply of funds, independence of savings and investment decisions, a constant marginal propensity to consume, and neutrality of expectations.

yields a plausible result.[1] Since it is easy to make approximate
estimates of the propensity to consume and the marginal
rate of taxation, the main source of difficulty is estimation
of the regional propensity to import (m). Brown points out
that the marginal *foreign import* content of a given change in
spending will not be less than 0·2, and since about one half
of consumption expenditure is probably mobile (i.e. could be
produced in or out of a given region) this yields a range of
0·2–0·7 for m. He suggests that 0·4 is a reasonable estimate
for the development areas; while Archibald, too, thinks that
a value of m of less than 0·4 is most unlikely. Archibald
consequently places the regional multiplier within the range
1·2–1·7,[2] while Brown's estimate (using a lower c but
making allowance for indirect taxes and transfer payments)
is 1·28. These estimates assume that the import content of the
autonomous injection is zero and ignore the repercussionary
effects of rising imports into a region on export demand in
other regions of the system. Taking account of the latter
effect gives an inter-regional multiplier, but Brown suggests
that given realistic values the value of the multiplier is raised
only slightly by allowing for induced exports.

The question of the import content of a given investment
injection is more serious; if we insert the above multiplier
estimates in the equation $\Delta Y = K \Delta I(1 - m_k)$, where $m_k =$
import content of investment, it is clear that m_k does not
have to be very high to reduce the net multiplier effect to
below unity. To be set against this is the possibility that the
investment injection will give rise to secondary induced
investment. Provided that the injection is sustained, and that

1. For examples see Archibald (1967) and Brown *et al.* (1967). Archibald's multiplier is $\dfrac{1}{1-(c-m)(1-t)}$ while Brown's is $\dfrac{1}{1-c(1-t_d-u)(1-m-t_i)}$, where $c=$ marginal propensity to consume, $m=$ marginal propensity to import, $t=$ marginal rate of taxation, $t_i=$ marginal rate of indirect taxation, $t_d=$ marginal rate of direct taxation, and u is the ratio of the fall in net transfer payments to the rise in income.

2. He assumes $c=0·9$.

there is no excess capacity in capital goods industries (to prevent a dampening of secondary investment expansion), secondary investment will be stimulated by a multiplier of $K(1-m_k)$. On similar lines, if the investment injection is associated with the entry of new firms into the region, this may shift the production functions of local firms and/or generate external economies. These points suggest the possible relevance of a *supermultiplier* (T. Wilson, 1968).[1] Although extremely difficult to forecast, this may be substantially higher than the standard multiplier.

It is possible, though the practical difficulties are serious, to derive the regional multiplier empirically. Archibald uses an indirect method to obtain a *minimum* value from national data. He summed the components of national household expenditure which *must* constitute local value added (L.V.A.) and, after adjusting from disposable income to G.N.P., thereby obtained an estimate for $(c-m)$ which sets a floor to the value added locally in any region. He assumed that all regions import all their food, primary fuel, manufactured and processed goods and that only their distribution added to L.V.A. He also took L.V.A. to be direct labour cost, adjusted for national insurance contributions. His result was a *minimum* multiplier of 1·21, an estimate equal to the lowest value derived by intuition.

Although covering himself by explicitly stating the objective as calculation of a minimum estimate, Archibald's method is not very useful. We often need to compare the size of the multiplier in one region with that of another, and an estimate from national data throws no light on this. The assumptions of no local expenditure on food or manufactured goods, and that labour cost is the only component of value added, are not very realistic. Finally as Archibald admits, the wage bill in many sectors responds only very slowly to local variations in demand.

1. The supermultiplier in a closed economy equals $\dfrac{1}{1-(c+v)}$ where $v=$ marginal propensity to invest. Modifying Archibald's multiplier to yield a supermultiplier we obtain $\dfrac{1}{1-(c-m)(1-t)-v(1-m_k)}$.

Much more useful is a direct method of verifying the size of the regional multiplier as suggested by Archibald himself. Consumers' expenditure patterns by commodity and region can be assessed from information in the Family Expenditure Survey. The main omission is the inability to estimate commodity origin (the marginal-propensity-to-import bogey again). In an interesting if not fully convincing paper, Steele (1969) has worked on the scanty data available to assign values to the ratio of imports to find demand in each region. His results show a range of 0·55–0·74, apart from 'perverse' estimates for Scotland (0·32 or 0·41).

Another possibility, though one in which I do not have much faith, is to estimate the propensity to import via a L.Q. technique analogous to the base methodology described above. We might assume that location quotients below unity in any sector imply that a region cannot supply its own needs and obtain an estimate of M/Y in employment terms by aggregating the 'deficit workers' for all such industries. Although as logical as any estimate of the export base by L.Q. methods, this does not give a meaningful estimate of the propensity to import. Since the sum of surplus workers equals the sum of deficit workers, the implication is that the propensity to import equals the ratio of base to over-all activity. This would only be true if regional trade was in balance, and there is no inherent reason why this should be so. A further inference is that the base multiplier is equal to the reciprocal of the propensity to import, an equality which would only hold if there were no net leakages through savings or taxes.[1] Since we know that $t = 0·2$ approximately, c would require a value of 1·2 for the equality to hold. This analysis shows up the weaknesses of the export base technique (or at least the L.Q. approach), but it does not offer much insight into estimating the propensity to import.

1. If $X=M$, then obviously $Y/X=1/m$ where $m=M/Y$.

Regional Business Cycles

Some approaches to the study of regional income fluctuations do not fall within the scope of inter-regional macroeconomics. An obvious example is the industry mix hypothesis which views regional cycles as the aggregate of the swings in individual industries and imputes to each regional industry the national cyclical change in activity in that industry. Regional cyclical experience not explained by industrial composition variable is treated as a residual. Since empirical evidence suggests that this residual is large (Borts, 1961; Garbarino, 1954; Neff, 1949) industry mix analysis is not fully satisfactory. Empirically based studies, however, have the advantage that they deal with dynamic influences which have cyclical significance, such as stochastic disturbances or inter-regional variations in the rate of innovation. These are not easily integrated into short-run income generation models.

Regional income models of the kind outlined earlier have some part to play in an analysis of regional fluctuations. The economic base concept is sometimes used in explaining regional cycles, but its disadvantages are as great as in applications of the base for regional income projections. It has the virtue of attracting attention to the importance of exports as a disequilibrating element in the regional economy. As the scale of economy declines exports tend to increase in importance, but emphasis of exports does not necessarily require the economic base approach. It is consistent with an industrial composition treatment since key export industries heavily engaged in inter-regional trade include capital goods and consumer durables, industrial groups which tend to be relatively unstable. It is also compatible with any regional cyclical model including inter-regional trade coefficients among its variables, such as inter-regional multiplier theory. But a comparative statics inter-regional multiplier merely gives a transmission mechanism and does not explain the origins of fluctuations.

However, the inter-regional multiplier can be an important element in regional business cycle theory if we make it dynamic.

One solution, as shown later, is to make allowance for induced investment and graft an accelerator on to the model. Another solution is to introduce inverse changes in autonomous expenditures in different regions. (Machlup, 1943, pp. 83–4, 161). This gives a pseudo-cycle[1] in one or more regions even if we retain a simple regional income model with no induced investment.

Consider a two-region model. With equal marginal propensities to consume in each region, and inverse changes in expenditure (e.g. in G) that are equal in absolute value, there will be no repercussion effect. However, if the inverse expenditure changes differ enough absolutely, then whether marginal propensities to consume are equal or not, there will be an initial wave in one region before it assumes the monotonic time path of national income (assuming that $c < 1$). For example, let us assume an increase in G in Region 1 but a much larger cut in spending in Region 2. Y_1 will initially expand, but this will be followed by a decline as the feedback effects of the larger fall in Y_2 on Region 1's exports assert themselves. In Region 2 and in the system as a whole, changes in income are negative and monotonic from the start. This is not a true cyclical model for the inverse expenditure changes are determined exogenously. However, if inverse expenditure changes were recurrent, it is conceptually possible for regional incomes to continue to fluctuate. Moreover, this approach shows how a region may be subject to cyclical swings in activity which are masked when we look at the course of national income.

Another method of analysing regional fluctuations which draws upon regional income theory was adopted by Vining (1948). He suggested a tool for estimating the cyclical sensitivity of a region. This is a measure of the elasticity of regional income in response to changes in exports (and hence, in an inter-regional framework, its responsiveness to changes in

1. Airov calls this pseudo-cycle a 'repercussion wave'. It is not a true cycle because income continues on a cyclical path for no more than one cycle then conforms to the time path of the nation and other regions.

income levels in other regions), i.e.

$$\frac{\text{percentage change in regional income}}{\text{percentage change in regional exports}}.$$

This is equal to $\dfrac{dY/Y}{dX/X}$

or $\dfrac{dY}{dX} \cdot \dfrac{X}{Y}$

and if we assume that $\dfrac{dY}{dX} = \dfrac{1}{1-(e-m)}$ and substitute

$Y - E + M$ for X we obtain

$$\frac{1-e'+m'}{1-e\ +m}$$

where e' is the average propensity to spend and m' is the average propensity to import.

If a region's expenditure and import functions are linear through the origin, this expression has a value of unity and regional income fluctuates precisely to the same degree as exports. In other cases, the higher the value of the above expression the more unstable is the region. For example, consider a case of two regions with equal and constant marginal propensities to spend and to import, but where in one region imports are a higher proportion of income (i.e. m' is larger). Then this latter region will be the more cyclically sensitive. The multiplier effect of a given reduction in exports will be the same in both regions, but the equilibrium level of income will fall most in the region with the higher m' because induced changes in income will represent a larger share of *local* income.

The value of m depends on the short-run income elasticities of demand for imports; the more inelastic is import demand the smaller is m, and *ceteris paribus* the greater is the cyclical sensitivity of the region. Inelastic import demand prevents the region from passing on the effects of income fluctuations to others. Finally, the greater the short-run income elasticities of demand for the exports of the region, the larger will be the change in exports from a given change in income in other regions (i.e. national income minus the income of the region in question). From information about the commodity distribution of imports and exports of a given region and from estimates of income elasticities of demand for individual products, it is possible to estimate broadly the income elasticities of demand for its exports and imports. However, the absence of inter-regional trade data in most countries makes it impossible to estimate the average and marginal propensities to import directly. In any event, although the Vining treatment enables something to be said about the relative stability of different regions, it falls far short of a comprehensive analysis of regional business cycles.

An Inter-regional Business Cycle Model

The most satisfactory methodological approach to regional fluctuations is the construction of inter-regional business cycles. These models are obtained by grafting international trade theory on to business cycle theory. The example below, merely used for illustrative purposes, modifies a multiplier-accelerator model to incorporate inter-regional trade in both consumption and investment goods.[1] We assume that the geographical pattern of this trade remains stable, that is, that as regional income levels change the inter-regional trade coefficients between each pair of regions remain constant.

We start from the basic regional income equation with the modification that we now use period analysis.

$$Y_i(t) = C_i(t) + I_i(t) + G_i(t) + X_i(t) - M_i(t). \qquad 21$$

Assume that consumption is a linear function of income in the preceding time period

$$C_i(t) = a_i + c_i Y_i(t-1). \qquad 22$$

1. For other types of model see Airov (1963).

Investment is treated as a linear function of the increase in total output.[1]

$$I_i(t) = I_i^a + b_i\{Y_i(t-1) - Y_i(t-2)\}. \qquad\qquad 23$$

I_i^a represents autonomous investment, and b_i is the constant ratio between the increase in capital stock and that in output with a lag, as indicated.

As before $G_i(t) = \bar{G_i}, \qquad\qquad\qquad\qquad\qquad\qquad 24$

and $\qquad\qquad A_i = a_i + I_i^a + \bar{G_i}. \qquad\qquad\qquad\qquad 25$

We add inter-regional trade in both consumers' and capital goods to the income generation model as follows:

$$X_i(t) = \sum_{j=1} m_{ij} Y_j(t-1) + \sum_{j=1} b_{ij}\{Y_j(t-1) - Y_j(t-2)\} \quad 26$$

$$M_i(t) = \sum_{j=1} m_{ji} Y_i(t-1) + \sum_{j=1} b_{ji}\{Y_i(t-1) - Y_i(t-2)\}. \quad 27$$

These equations assume that in inter-regional trade capital goods refer only to induced investment, and that autonomous investment expenditures are domestically generated.[2]

1. The alternative is to make investment a function of consumption. However, the assumption chosen is reasonable since capital goods are required to increase the output of investment goods as well as consumption goods.

2. It is clear that domestic investment
$$I_i^D(t) = I_i^a(t) + b_i\{Y_i(t-1) - Y_i(t-2)\}$$
$$- \sum_{j=1} b_{ji}\{Y_i(t-1) - Y_i(t-2)\},$$

and that domestic consumption
$$C_i^D(t) = a_i + c_i Y_i(t-1) - \sum_{j=1} m_{ji} Y_i(t-1).$$

Substituting equations **22–27** into **21** we obtain:

$$Y_i(t) = A_i + \left[c_i + b_i - \left(\sum_{j=1} m_{ji} + \sum_{j=1} b_{ji} \right) \right] Y_i(t-1)$$

$$- \left(b_i - \sum_{j=1} b_{ji} \right) Y_i(t-2) + \left(\sum_{j=1} m_{ij} + \sum_{j=1} b_{ij} \right) Y_j(t-1)$$

$$- \sum_{j=1} b_{ij} \, Y_j(t-2). \qquad \textbf{28}$$

Thus, regional income is a function of previous domestic expenditures and of the previous income levels in other regions of the system. If equilibrium is disturbed by a change in autonomous expenditures in Region i or any other region of the system then the time path of regional income may, given appropriate values to the expenditure and trading coefficients, be cyclical.

This inter-regional business cycle model may be compared with its parallel in the national economy. Since national income is the sum of regional incomes we may write

$$Y(t) = \sum_{i=1} Y_i(t), \qquad \textbf{29}$$

and if we assume that the nation is a closed economy then

$$\sum_{i=1} X_i = \sum_{i=1} M_i; \qquad \textbf{30}$$

that is

$$\sum_{i=1} \sum_{j=1} m_{ij} \, Y_j(t-1) + \sum_{i=1} \sum_{j=1} b_{ij} \{ Y_j(t-1) - Y_j(t-2) \} =$$

$$\sum_{i=1} \sum_{j=1} m_{ji} \, Y_i(t-1) + \sum_{i=1} \sum_{j=1} b_{ji} \{ Y_i(t-1) - Y_i(t-2) \}.$$

Cancelling out inter-regional trade we obtain

$$Y(t) = \sum_{i=1} A_i + \sum_{i=1} (c_i + b_i) \, Y_i(t-1) - \sum_{i=1} b_i \, Y_i(t-2) \quad \textbf{31a}$$

or $$Y(t) = A + (c+b)\,Y(t-1) - b\,Y(t-2), \qquad \textbf{31b}$$

where A represents national autonomous expenditures, c is the national marginal propensity to consume and b is the national marginal capital–output ratio.

Reverting to the inter-regional model, the interesting questions are whether the parameters of the model are likely to have values that will lead to fluctuations and, assuming a disturbance to equilibrium income in one or more regions, what is the nature of the time paths followed by income in each region? To deal with the second question first, the regional system in an advanced economy is probably indecomposable; in this context this means that each region trades directly or indirectly with every region. The mathematical solution is consequently obtained by solving one system of simultaneous difference equations. In such a system, the same roots appear in the solution of the time path of income in every region, and these time paths have a common qualitative character. If the structural coefficients are of a magnitude that gives rise to cycles, the periodicity of cycles in each region and in the nation will be the same. However, the amplitude of fluctuations will vary from region to region depending on (a) the relative size of c_i and b_i, (b) the values of the inter-regional trade coefficients and (c) stochastic disturbances.

Will cycles result from this model? There are too many coefficients for us to discover in advance the parametric combinations which will give rise to fluctuations so we have to proceed by partial experiments.[1] Three examples for the simplest case of a two-region model are given in Table 1 overleaf.

To obtain cycles of constant amplitude or damped cycles we have to assign unrealistically low values to the parameters in the equations, especially to the capital coefficients. Even in case 2 where the accelerators are weak the cycles which emerge are explosive. In case 3 where we do obtain damped

1. There is no similar device to Samuelson's parametric map used to determine the nature of the time path in national multiplier-accelerator models.

Table 1
Structural Coefficients and Time Paths of Income in a
Two-Region Multiplier-Accelerator Model

Nature of time path =	Explosive growth	Explosive cycles	Damped cycles
	case 1	case 2	case 3
c_1	0·9	0·8	0·5
c_2	0·9	0·8	0·3
m_{12}	0·4	0·3	0·1
m_{21}	0·5	0·2	0·2
b_1	2·0	1·25	1·2
b_2	2·5	1·0	1·0
b_{12}	0·5	0·6	0·5
b_{21}	1·0	0·25	0·2

cycles all the structural coefficients are extremely low. If we
wish to retain the multiplier-accelerator model and obtain
realistic (i.e. non-explosive) cyclical paths we must either
introduce buffers (full employment, regional capacity constraints, bottlenecks in the supply of investment funds, etc.)
or relax the assumption of constant government expenditures
and permit changes in spending for stabilization purposes.

2 Regional Growth

Introduction

The main difference between the analysis of growth in the national economy and in regions is the emphasis in the latter on factor movements. It is often permissible, if incomplete, to treat the nation as a closed economy. This assumption can never be made for regions. The possibility of inflows and outflows of labour and capital widen substantially the range within which regional growth rates differ, even with a given national stock of resources. Since, in a truly dynamic analysis, this stock will itself be increasing, the growth rate in a region can be far higher than normally achieved by a national economy or, at the other extreme, be negative. Negative growth rates in total output are only very rarely found in an advanced national economy. However, as resource flows may be equilibrating, it does not follow that growth differentials between regions will necessarily be wider than between countries.

There are two quite different methodological approaches to regional growth: adaptation of macroeconomic models used in aggregate growth theory (and special regional variants such as export base theory) or interpretation of a region's growth in terms of the dynamics of industrial structure. These approaches are complementary. We shall concentrate on the first, partly because it follows on naturally from inter-regional macroeconomic analysis, partly because it enables us to identify the crucial links between factor movements and regional growth more clearly. However, the industrial structure approach analyses the changing pattern of regional growth as the net effect of the location and output decisions of business firms in response to changes in input and market requirements in their industries (input–output access[1]), and factor flows are relevant variables in such decisions.

A common procedure for 'industrial structure-regional growth' analysis is to consider the region as a weighted representation of a set of national industries, to assign national rates of growth to these industries regardless of where they are located, and to test whether a region's actual growth performance can be explained by this industrial composition effect (*proportional shifts*). If the residual is large, then regional growth cannot be understood without referring to 'within region' considerations – why industries grow faster (or slower) in some regions than in the national economy (*differential shifts*). Tests on long-run historical data in the United States by Perloff and his associates (1960, Part IV), by Borts and Stein (1964, pp. 44–7) and for shorter periods in Britain by Mrs Hemming (1963) and Stilwell (1969) have shown that the residual is often large.[2] Mackay (1968) has recently argued that the proportional shift represents only a *minimum* estimate of the influence of industrial structure. Because all industries in the regional economy are interdependent, the effects of a very favourable or highly unfavourable industrial composition will affect the performance of other sectors by secondary multiplier effects on service industries and by technological linkages with supplying industries.

Elements of regional growth which are estimated in the residual often reflect the influence of industrial structure. But does this require us to abandon the proportionality and differential shift technique? The main point of the technique is to enable us to separate extraregional and 'within region' elements of regional growth. If the technological linkages of lead industries exist at the national level they will be accounted

1. This concept used by Perloff, Dunn, Lampard and Muth (1960) refers to the balance between locational advantages and disadvantages of a particular region for a given industry, where these advantages and disadvantages are interpreted in terms of access to either internal or external markets and to inputs and other supply factors.

2. In addition, Stilwell subtracts from the differential shift the 'proportionality modification' shift. This measures the impact on regional growth of *changes* in industrial composition over the period of observation.

for, if our industrial disaggregation is fine enough, in the composition effect. If the linkages and the multiplier effects are purely local then their impact *should* be included in the residual, since a high residual simply draws our attention to growth influences specific to the region.

This attack on the industrial structure approach is therefore misconceived. Nevertheless, analysis of the relationship between industrial structure and regional growth can only go so far. It can only throw light on changes in the volume of economic activity and offers little insight into changes in regional *per capita* incomes. Moreover, it is little more than a set of techniques for assembling and ordering data, and falls far short of a theory of growth. For the latter, inter-regional macroeconomics is more fruitful.

The Harrod—Domar Model in a Regional System

The Harrod—Domar growth model can be adapted for regional growth analysis by allowing for inter-regional movements of capital and labour. We start from the specific assumptions of the model; a constant propensity to save (s), fixed coefficients in production, and a constant rate of growth in the labour force (n, where n = the rate of population growth).[1] For steady growth equilibrium conditions have to be satisfied for both inputs, (i.e. $g = k = n$, where g = rate of growth of output, and k = rate of growth of capital). In equilibrium, planned saving must continuously equal planned investment. Thus, for

k we may write $\dfrac{I}{K} = \dfrac{S}{K} = \dfrac{S}{Y} \cdot \dfrac{Y}{K} = \dfrac{s}{v}.$

where v is the capital–output ratio. Steady growth requires that $g = n = s/v$. Since s, v and n are all determined independently, steady growth can result only by chance.

1. Other assumptions are a single-good economy, constant returns to scale and no technical progress. For a more extended discussion of the Harrod—Domar model in a non-regional setting see Harrod (1948) and Domar (1957). For a brief summary see Ackley (1961, pp. 513–29).

But regions are open economies. Imports are leakages as well as savings, exports, as well as investment, can fill the gap between domestic consumption and full capacity output, and excess savings can be diverted to other regions by running an export surplus. Moreover, if a region's population is increasing too fast to be absorbed into employment at the current growth rate, net migration may help to balance n and g.

The static condition for an open economy

$$S + M = I + X \qquad\qquad 32$$

can be rewritten as

$$(s + m) Y = I + X \qquad\qquad 33a$$

or

$$\frac{I}{Y} = s + m - \frac{X}{Y}. \qquad\qquad 33b$$

We know that a region's exports X_t can be expressed in terms of the imports of other regions as

$$\sum_{j=1} M_{ij} = \sum_{j=1} m_{ij} Y_j.$$

Thus the growth equation for a region can be rewritten as:

$$g_i = \frac{s_i + m_i - \displaystyle\sum_{j=1} m_{ij} Y_j / Y_i}{v_i}. \qquad\qquad 34$$

Capital may still grow at the same rate as output in a region even if savings tend to exceed investment provided the savings–investment gap is closed by running an export surplus.[1]

1. For the system as a whole, the constraint is that total inter-regional trade must balance, i.e.

$$\sum_{i=1} \sum_{j=1} M_{ij} = \sum_{i=1} \sum_{j=1} M_{ij}.$$

Similarly, excess labour can be soaked up by out-migration or labour shortage met by immigration from other regions of the system.[1] The requirement for equilibrium is that

$$g_i = n_i \pm r_i, \qquad\qquad 35$$

where r is the rate of migration expressed as the net number of out- or in-migrants (R_i) in each time period as a percentage of the region's population (P_i). From the viewpoint of the

system as a whole, $\quad r_i = \dfrac{R_i}{P_i} = \dfrac{\sum\limits_{j=1} R_{ij}}{P_i},$

subject to $\quad \sum\limits_{i=1} \sum\limits_{j=1} R_{ij} = 0.$

Although the conditions for steady growth in a single region are somewhat less restrictive than in the closed economy case, steady growth may still be the exception rather than the rule. Moreover, the attainment of equilibrium conditions in one region may alter the requirements of equilibrium in others, and this will have further repercussions on its own growth rate. Steady growth in each constituent region of the system cannot be predicted from the model as it stands. Whether or not there will be a tendency to steady growth depends on whether or not inter-regional flows of capital and labour are equilibrating, and these are not determined within the model. To answer this question we have to feed into the model a theory of resource mobility. This will be discussed later.

The absence of an automatic equilibrating mechanism in the Harrod–Domar model requires us to examine briefly what happens when regional growth rates depart from an equilibrium path. If the equilibrium growth rate in Region i is higher than in other regions, then g_i must rise continuously over time. This is because if $g_i > g_j$ ($j = 1, 2, \ldots, n$) then Y_j/Y_i becomes smaller, and in equation 34

$$\frac{\sum\limits_{j=1} m_{ij} Y_j}{Y_i}$$

becomes smaller with the result that g_i rises. Thus, in this model

1. Another variable which may make the conditions for full employment equilibrium less restrictive is a change in activity rates.

if regional growth rates initially differ, the divergence is likely to become wider in the absence of equilibrating factor flows.

Regions will grow faster the higher their propensities to save and the lower their capital–output ratios. However, net capital imports are additions to a region's aggregate savings. Consequently, regions with net import surpluses, i.e. where

$$m_i - \frac{\sum\limits_{j=1} m_{ij}\, Y_j}{Y_i} > 0,$$ can grow faster than other regions.

Similarly, regions experiencing net immigration will also grow faster than others. As we have seen, for steady growth capital and labour must both grow at the same rate; this follows from the assumption of fixed coefficients. Unless fast-growing regions have very high savings rates and high rates of natural increase, the Harrod–Domar model predicts that they are likely to import *both* capital *and* labour.

Neo-Classical Models

Neo-classical growth models have been used widely in regional analysis. (See, for example, Borts (1960), Borts and Stein (1964) and Romans (1965).) Nevertheless, some of their assumptions are inappropriate. The assumption of continuous full employment is often inapplicable to a multiregional system in which regional problems emerge because of geographical differences in the degree of resource utilization. Similarly, the assumption of perfect competition is out of place in the space economy where oligopoly, pure monopoly or monopolistic competition are more typical market structures. The neo-classical model attracts the regional economist because it implies a theory of factor mobility in addition to a theory of growth. The implication of perfect competition is that capital and labour move in response to differentials in factor returns.

The conditions of steady growth in a neo-classical model are less restrictive than in the Harrod–Domar model because of the possibility of substitution between capital and labour, and hence flexibility in the capital–output ratio. The rate of growth is composed of three sources: capital accumulation, an increase in labour supply and a residual, which we may call technical progress, but which includes everything which improves the efficiency of a given stock of resources. If we assume that the rate of technical progress is a function of time, then we may derive from the production function[1]

$$Y_i = f_i (K, L, t) \qquad\qquad 36$$

the growth equation

$$y_i = a_i k_i + (1-a_i) n_i + T_i; \qquad\qquad 37$$

where y, k, n, and T are the growth rates of output, capital, labour and technical progress respectively, a = capital's share of income (or the marginal product of capital $\frac{\Delta Y}{\Delta K} \times \frac{K}{Y}$) and if we assume constant returns to scale $(1-a)$ = labour's income share (i.e. $\frac{\Delta Y}{\Delta L} \times \frac{L}{Y}$).

The neo-classical model requires full capacity growth, and this in turn requires a mechanism to equate investment with full employment savings. The rate of interest (m) is such a mechanism. An equilibrium requirement is that m = the rate of profit which, in this model, is the marginal product of capital MPK_i. Thus steady growth requires that

$$MPK_i = a_i \frac{Y_i}{K_i} = m. \qquad\qquad 38$$

If m is given, Y and K must grow at the same rate if a is to remain constant. Thus for steady growth y_i must equal k_i. Substituting y_i in equation 37 we obtain

$$y_i = \frac{T_i}{1-a_i} + n_i \qquad\qquad 39$$

and for steady growth in the system as a whole $\left(\dfrac{T_i}{1-a_i} + n_i\right)$ must be equal to $\left(\dfrac{T_j}{1-a_j} + n_j\right)$ where $j = 1, 2, .., n-i$. However, inter-regional differences in the rates of technical progress and population growth may be offset by different capital–output ratios (which lead to changes in a). This adjust-

1. The derivation is well known. For a clear demonstration see Meade (1961, pp. 8–12).

ability in K/Y is the key feature of neo-classical models.

An equilibrium condition for the whole system is that $\sum_{i=1} I_i = \sum_{i=1} S_i$. But internally generated savings in the individual region do not have to be equal to regional investment. A region will import capital if its rate of growth of capital is greater than the ratio of domestic savings to capital. Since $S_i = s_i Y_i$ and $I_i = k_i K_i$ then Region i will import capital if

$$k_i > \frac{s_i}{v_i} \qquad\qquad 40$$

where $v_i = K_i/Y_i$. The inequality of **40** can hold only if $(m_i - \sum_{j=1} m_{ij} Y_j)/Y_i$ is positive, that is if Region i runs an import surplus. Thus, as with the Harrod–Domar model, the higher a region's growth rate the more likely that it will import capital.

The main difference between the neo-classical and the Harrod–Domar approaches to the analysis of regional growth is, as suggested above, that neo-classicism implies a theory of factor mobility. This can be explained most clearly in comparative statics terms. Let us assume: two regions; a single homogeneous good; zero transport costs; a fixed supply of labour and no technical progress; perfect competition, and identical production functions in each region taking the form $Y = f(K, L)$ and subject to constant returns to scale. The last assumption makes the marginal products of labour, MPL, direct and the marginal products of capital, MPK, inverse functions of the capital–labour ratio (K/L). Given perfect competition, MPL equals the real wage.

Because each region produces a homogeneous output with identical production functions, the region with the higher K/L has the higher real wage and the lower MPK while the region with the lower K/L has the lower real wage but the higher MPK. This will not be an equilibrium situation in the system as a whole. For equilibrium, capital will flow from high to low wage regions, since the latter offer higher returns to capital and labour will flow in opposite direction until factor returns are equalized. Low-wage, low-income regions should therefore grow faster than other regions, enjoying higher rates of capital accumulation and greater increases in wages. As a result, there should be a convergence process in regional *per capita* incomes. This is the opposite prediction to that of the pure Harrod–Domar model where if the conditions for steady growth are not satisfied the most likely result is a widening of regional growth rates.

The weakness of this theory of resource mobility is that we cannot be sure that its predictions will hold if we drop the comparative statics assumptions. In dynamic analysis, we must allow for regional variations in internal rates of growth of labour supply and technical progress. Rapid natural increase in low-wage regions may prevent rising incomes, and shifts to the right in the MPK function in high-wage regions due to technical change may mean that capital flows into rather than out of these regions. Even within the framework of the comparative statics model, high-wage regions may still grow fastest if we drop the assumptions of regionally identical production functions and a single commodity. In the first case increasing capital intensity could offset the dampening effects of in-migration on wage levels, while in the second demand shifts may favour the export sectors of high-income regions.

Other difficulties are: (1) that factors may not move in response to differences in returns (this is particularly the case with labour) or may move for other reasons, and (2) that resource mobility cannot be comprehensively analysed within a two-factor model. Convergence in regional growth is consequently an open question. It is nevertheless important, and requires further discussion.

Export Base Models

Export base models have received some attention as explanations of long-run growth as well as of short-run income change.[1] They imply that the growth of a region depends upon the growth of its export industries and that expansion in

1. For a controversy on their importance see North (1955) and Tiebout (1956). See also Perloff, Dunn, Lampard and Muth (1960, ch. 4) and Thomas (1964).

demand external to the region is the main determinant of regional growth. The limitations of this approach are if anything greater than in comparative statics analysis: the neglect of autonomous variables other than exports, particularly in a dynamic context; the neglect of technical change and autonomous investment; the assumption that exports are exogenously determined whereas we have seen that in inter-regional trade the level of exports is determined by the import functions of other regions; the export base becomes a less reliable indicator of regional growth as the scale of region increases.

It is true that supporters of the export base theory have, in response to criticism, recognized that regions may grow as a result of influences other than export expansion: central government spending in the region; in-migration caused by non-economic forces; import-substitution in local industries; and increased efficiency in local supplying industries. But in general they regard investment in local industries as being induced by an expansion in income received from outside the region. The export base approach is of most value when we interpret it loosely by stressing the importance of changing national demand patterns in regional growth and the dependence of a region's growth rate upon the growth performance of the national economy.

The predictions of the export base hypothesis are different from those of other models of regional growth. An expansion in a region's export base (i.e. its gross exports) will tend to lead to a higher growth rate. Fast-growing regions will consequently tend to run export surpluses, unless the expansion in exports is outweighed by higher induced imports – a condition of which is that the marginal propensity to spend > 1. A second difference is that export base theory does not imply an equilibrium rate of growth.[1] If regions have excess capacity and unemployment, an expansion in the base will boost regional growth without difficulty; on the other hand, if there is continuous full employment an export surplus would mean a withdrawal of savings from the region and a dampening of the growth rate. However, regions enjoying export base ex-

pansion are likely to import labour. A third difference is that
the export base theory says nothing about whether regional
growth rates are likely to converge or diverge. If the system is a
closed one, it is clear that not all regions can have export
surpluses and grow rapidly. But the possibility of convergence
depends on whether or not low income regions are the areas
most likely to raise their rate of exports. Export base models
do not throw any light on the possibility of a relationship
between levels of income and export capacity.

Is Convergence Inevitable ?

It is important to consider whether the pattern of regional
growth in a free market leads to a convergence in regional *per
capita* incomes and the strength of such a convergence tendency if it exists. The answer to this question may dictate how
necessary it is to have a regional policy, and how active
intervention needs to be. Since growth models differ in their
predictions about the likelihood of convergence, the question
can only be settled empirically. Here we shall do no more than
list the factors making for and inhibiting convergence.

There are three important potential convergence forces.
Firstly, there is the possibility of equilibrating factor flows as
predicted by the neo-classical model. Labour will move from
low- to high-wage regions and, if wages and the marginal product of capital are inversely correlated, capital will flow in the
opposite direction. Consequently, low-wage regions should
grow fastest. A second major source of convergence is reallocation of resources within regions from low-wage sectors
(such as agriculture) to high-productivity, high-wage sectors,
thereby raising average incomes per head. In many countries,
much of regional variations in income per head may be traced
to different proportions of resources employed in agriculture.
The scope for internal reallocation of this kind is greater in
agrarian low-wage regions. Thirdly, maturity characteristics
in long-established high-income regions may slow down future
increases in *per capita* incomes. The most important of these

characteristics are probably exhaustion of the scope for inter-sectoral resource shifts and inelastic labour supply functions (because of low net reproduction rates in highly urbanized regions).

There is nothing inevitable about these convergence forces, apart from the second which may at times proceed very slowly. Instead, divergence forces may predominate. In particular, in a dynamic framework factor movements may be disequilibrating. It is true that if labour migrates, the net movement will usually be from low- to high-wage regions, even though increased employment opportunities rather than higher wages may provide the motive. However, it is uncertain whether such migration will narrow regional income differentials. Investment in migration may be unprofitable especially for older workers because of the costs involved in changing residences and jobs, and therefore migration may be insufficient to have much impact on regional wage levels. In some circumstances migration may be disequilibrating. For example, there may be increasing returns to scale in the industries of destination regions. Moreover, in-migration not only affects wages but also consumption levels, the degree of utilization of social capital and investment; as a result, in-migration may raise the demand for labour by more than it contributes to labour supply.

When we relax the assumptions of comparative statics models and allow for technical progress and geographical concentration in managers and technical personnel, capital is liable to flow in the wrong direction for convergence. High-income regions benefit from agglomeration economies which are self-sustaining. Innovations and technical progress do not spread evenly and rapidly over space but frequently cluster in prosperous regions; for instance, technical progress may be a function of the levels of R and D expenditures which are higher in high-income regions. Empirical observation of innovational routes suggests that they are often diffused down the urban hierarchy so that highly urbanized regions gain disproportionately. The recipients of new techniques, that is high-calibre managers, tend to be disproportionately concentrated in wealthy metropolitan regions and are often unwilling to move to less-developed regions suffering from inferior social and cultural environments. Finally, if technical progress is embodied in capital accumulation, rich regions may benefit because of higher levels of investment and an industry mix favourable to technological advance.

Apart from technical progress, high-income regions may have other advantages. The presence of external economies in or near metropolitan centres may continue to attract a large share of economic expansion. Locational shifts in industry may favour high-income regions because of their relative *input–output access* advantages. Changes in national demand may also favour these regions if they have an industrial composition heavily weighted with high income elasticity of demand industries. For all these reasons, continuous shifts to the right in the marginal product of the capital function may more than compensate for its negative slope. Finally, we must allow for imperfections in the capital market. Even if prospective returns were higher in low-income regions, capital may not flow there. A high proportion of national savings will tend to be generated in high-income regions. There may be some preference for investing in the home region either because of psychic income elements or as a result of overestimation of the risks in underdeveloped regions.

Even if factor flows were equilibrating and other convergence tendencies were strong, regional *per capita* incomes would not be fully equalized. In the first place, even if returns to homogeneous factors are equalized, inter-regional wage differentials will remain because of non-homogeneity characteristics: differences in occupational distribution, the proportion of skilled workers, industrial composition, the degree of urbanization and other aspects of regional employment structure (age, sex, colour, etc.). Secondly, *per capita* income differences may remain because of regional variations in activity rates due to regional differences in unemployment and in the labour-force-population ratio. In the United and in the labour-force–population ratio. In the United States, the dispersion of activity rates between regions has been reduced over time, and this has been one element in convergence. Finally, property income may be disproportionately concentrated on some regions, because the residences of property owners will not be equally distributed over all parts of the country.

Empirical Evidence

Data limitations make it difficult, and in many cases impossible at present to test the predictive power of alternative models of regional growth. It is quite possible on the basis of theoretical analysis alone to argue that the inter-regional growth process leads to convergence or to divergence, according to the emphasis given to particular variables. But we cannot even come to provisional conclusions without empirical analysis. The regional growth models we have described yield testable hypotheses (as shown in Table 2), and only the absence of data prevents our testing them. Instead we shall have to be satisfied with casual empirical observations. On the other hand, we have seen that there are influences on convergence other than those accounted for in these models, and on this question – whether regional growth rates converge or not – there is more scope for empirical analysis.

Table 2
Predictions of Regional Growth Models

| | *Characteristics of Fast-Growing Regions* | | | |
Model	*Level of income*	*Direction of labour*	*Direction of capital*	*Inter-regional growth*
Harrod–Domar	high	in	in	divergence
Neo-classical	low	out	in	convergence
Export base (no capacity constraint)	?	in	out	?

Convergence: United States

Income data by States have been available for many years in
the United States, and several studies have given clear support
to the convergence hypothesis.[1] As shown in Tables 3 and 4
there has been marked convergence since 1880 not only in
total *per capita* income but in individual income components
with the exception of proprietors' income. However, the convergence process was unsteady and occasionally reversed itself
– as in the 1920s. Equalization was far from complete and the
rank order of States by *per capita* income changed little. Moreover, high-income regions were pulled down towards the
national average, rather than low-income regions being pulled
up.

The main sources of convergence were increasing similarity
in State ratios of the non-agricultural–total labour force
(i.e. improvement in *intra*regional resource allocation) and
declining inter-regional differences in property income *per
capita*. The distribution of property income was very unequal,
but its influence on total *per capita* income was relatively
small (since it accounted for only one eighth of total personal
income). Inter-regional factor movements were not a major
factor in convergence, though immigration into high-income
regions held their *per capita* income growth in check. Migration did not reduce markedly the initial dispersion of relative
wages, for the convergence in inter-regional wage differentials
within non-agricultural sectors and *within* agriculture was very
weak.

Table 3
Coefficient of Variation (%) in *Per Capita* Personal Income,
Nine Major Regions of the United States, 1880–1950

1880	1900	1919–20	1949–51
57·9	42·5	30·4	23·4

Source: Easterlin (1960).

1. See Easterlin (1958 and 1960), Hanna (1957 and 1959), Perloff
et al. (1960, Part V), Borts and Stein (1964), Romans (1965), Smolensky (1961), Schwartz and Graham (1956), Bjork (1968), Williamson
(1965).Williamson's study is important for its international comparisons.

Table 4
Coefficient of Variation (%) of State *Per Capita* Income
(Total and Components), United States in 1929 and 1951

	Total	Wages and salaries	Transfer payments	Proprietors' income	Property income
1929	35·2	39·9	44·0	27·6	71·9
1951	22·2	29·1	17·4	43·6	40·7

Source: Hanna (1959).

Convergence? – Great Britain

There are no suitable regional income estimates for Great Britain. The only data we have were collected by the Inland Revenue Department for tax purposes, and are subject to severe qualifications.[1] In addition, regional definitions have changed over the period for which data are available; I have reconstructed the statistics for 1949/50 and 1959/60 from county estimates to bring them into line with the new standard regions, but certain arbitrary assumptions had to be made for counties divided between two or more regions.

The relevant material has been assembled in Table 5. There is no clear indication of convergence over the period. The coefficient of variation in fact rose in the 1950s, though it fell in the early 1960s – perhaps reflecting the more activist regional policies of recent years – but the changes in the coefficient were small. As can be seen from the final column of Table 5 the range of increase in incomes over the period 1950–65 was very narrow. Some low-income regions increased their

1. These defects are well known: (1) data are published only at five year intervals; (2) low incomes are excluded with different exemption limits in particular years (rising from £135 to £275); (3) the regional distribution of civil servants, armed forces and merchant seamen is excluded; (4) average incomes refer to per tax-paying unit rather than per head of population (and married couples count as one unit); (5) incomes are assessed at place of business, not place of residence; this defect is acute for investment income, since company profits of multiplant firms will normally be assigned to the region where the company headquarters is located.

income lével rapidly (e.g. Wales) while in others (e.g. Scotland) the expansion was below average. A test of the hypothesis that low-income regions exhibited above average increases in incomes yielded a rank correlation coefficient which was statistically insignificant. The rank orders show slight changes over the period with Yorkshire and Scotland slipping while the South-West and East Anglia rose in rank.

Table 5
Regional Income Per Tax-Paying Unit, 1949/50, 1959/60 and 1964/5 (Great Britain)

	1949/50 (£)	1959/60 (£)	1964/5 (£)	Percentage increase in money income per unit, 1949/50–1964/5
South-East	430	794	1085	152
West Midlands	395	752	1024	159
East Midlands	391	723	980	151
South-West	374	694	968	159
Yorkshire and Humberside	393	709	962	145
North-West	380	709	960	153
East Anglia	373	669	951	155
Scotland	380	674	937	147
Wales	356	678	933	162
Northern	369	686	927	151
Great Britain	399	734	1007	152
Coefficient of variation (%)	15·7	16·6	14·9	
Lowest income as % of highest income	82·8	84·3	85·4	

Rank correlation coefficient between level of income (1949/50, ranked in ascending order) and rate of growth of income per tax-paying unit 1949/50 – 1964/5 (ranked from greatest to smallest increase), $\rho = 0.315$ (statistically insignificant).
Source: Inland Revenue Reports.

The percentage gap between the poorest and the richest region narrowed steadily. Nevertheless, the convergence hypothesis is not supported. Perhaps the period is too short to reveal the trend. Another difficulty is that the data refer to money incomes, and we have no regional cost-of-living data to show whether the variation in *real* incomes has the same distribution. Of course, one reason why convergence tendencies in Britain may be weak is the fact that the gap between low and high income regions is so small.[1]

Suggestions for Testing Regional Growth Models

As shown in Table 2 above, the growth models we have discussed throw up certain hypotheses about the relationship between a region's growth, its level of income, and the direction of capital movements and migration. A thorough analysis of the regional growth process would need to test these hypotheses. Unfortunately the data on which these tests might be made do not yet exist. As we have seen, our statistics on regional income levels are very imperfect. We can obtain detailed information on population growth from *Censuses of Population* and the Registrar General's reports, but the migration estimates are less reliable and have to be treated with some caution. We lack indicators of regional growth, and we are completely in the dark about inter-regional capital movements.

However, it might be conceptually feasible to estimate the direction of net capital flows indirectly, via a comparison of regional savings with regional investment. Abstracting from international capital flows, a region will import capital if its share in national investment is higher than its share of national savings, and vice versa. But this indirect solution only throws us up against the data barrier again, since there are no estimates of regional savings and investment. Nevertheless, this methodology is worth stating since we shall certainly have estimates of regional savings and investment long before we obtain direct information about capital movements as a whole.

1. Myrdal (1957) has argued that regional income differences are much narrower in advanced than in less-developed economies.

For the provisional observations made here, we have to rely on crude imperfect proxies. Thus, for an index of regional growth we have to use estimates of growth in employment. As a proxy for a region's share in national savings we assume that for high-income regions this share is not less than their share in personal income and for low-income regions not greater than their personal income share.[1] For regional investment shares we use as proxies (a) the regional distribution of construction orders and (b) regional shares in industrial building completions (1960–65). These two indicators show similar results, though a drawback is that they refer only to investment in building and works.[2] Where these proxies for investment and savings shares differ markedly, we are able to identify whether the region imports or exports capital.[3]

The tentative results of this inquiry are given in Table 6. In column 4, for two regions the investment and savings shares were too close together (given the imperfections of the proxies) to identify the direction of capital flows, and the question marks in three cases indicate that the evidence is not overwhelmingly conclusive. There is no unambiguous support for any one of the growth models examined earlier. The neoclassical model gives the best fit. Several low-income regions

1. Change in investment income might be a reasonable proxy for savings were it not for the fatal defect about the regional allocation of investment income mentioned above. Another possibility is that a region's share in tax payments might be used as a substitute for its share in savings because the tax share reflects the *distribution* of income in a region.

2. Taylor (1967) has suggested that industrial consumption of electricity might be used as a proxy for the capital stock in plant and equipment. Apart from criticisms of this proxy (see Heathfield and Hilton, 1968), it could not be adopted in our analysis because the Area Electricity Boards differ so much from the new standard regions. A. J. Brown *et al.* (1968) present data on non-consumption expenditures per head. These too could not be used for our purposes, partly because they refer to the old standard regions but primarily because non-consumption expenditures are estimated residually and include not only gross capital formation and public expenditure but also net regional exports.

3. A capital importing region may import capital from abroad rather than from other regions. Scotland may fall into this category.

(Wales, Yorkshire, Scotland and Northern) imported capital and exported labour. Their modest employment growth cannot necessarily be regarded as unchallengeable evidence of slow growth since employment growth is likely to be damped in emigrant regions. However, personal income grew more slowly than the average in the Northern and Yorkshire regions, 1959/60–1964/5. Conversely, two high-income regions (the South-East and the East Midlands) imported labour and probably exported capital which is also consistent with neo-classical theory. But these two regions grew faster than average according to the employment index (though personal income in both cases increased no more than average). Apart from the defects of the growth index, the lack of correspondence between equilibrating factor flows and growth performance may simply mean that factor movements have not been sufficiently large. Another qualification is that capital has not flowed from high-income to low-income regions in a freely competitive market. Subsidies have raised the rate of return on investment in development regions while negative controls have frequently prevented the domestic employment of capital in the high-income regions.

Some of the evidence is consistent with other models. The South-East and East Midlands experience is also compatible with export base theory, and indeed it is plausible that both these regions prosper primarily by supplying goods and services to other regions. On the other hand, East Anglia and the West Midlands appear to have imported both capital and labour and to have grown rapidly. This is more consistent with a Harrod–Domar type of analysis than either of the other two models. However, *a priori* reasoning would suggest that in fast-growing regions new investment opportunities and a growing demand for labour will require *both* capital *and* labour from outside. Other models of regional growth could be constructed to fit this case. The models we have examined are merely examples. A more rigorous testing of these and other models must await the accumulation of more useful data on regional growth, savings and investment.

Table 6
Regional Growth Performance and Direction of Factor
Flows in Great Britain

	(1) Growth: percentage increase in employment 1959–65	(2) Level of Income	(3) Labour:[1] net migration 1956–66 as a percentage of 1956 population	(4) Capital
East Anglia	fast (11·2)	low	in (+5·7)	in?
West Midlands	fast (10·1)	high	in (+2·4)	in?
South-East	fast (9·5)	high	in (+3·3)	out
South-West	fast (10·1)	low	in (+5·8)	—
East Midlands	fast (9·5)	high	in (+2·6)	out?
Wales	slow (5·9)	low	out (−0·6)	in
Yorkshire and Humberside	slow (5·4)	low	out (−1·4)	in
North-West	slow (2·7)	low	out (−1·0)	—
Scotland	slow (2·7)	low	out (−5·7)	in
Northern	slow (2·4)	low	out (−2·2)	in

Sources: 1. Department of Employment and Productivity data (G.B.=7·6%).
2. *Inland Revenue Reports* for 1959/60 and 1964/5.
3. *Census of Population* data and Registrar General's estimates.
4. Various (see text), but mainly *Abstract of Regional Statistics*.

1. The demographic position of Wales, the North-West and Yorkshire and Humberside has improved markedly since 1961. In recent years, Wales has in fact been gaining slightly from migration.

Part Two The Nodal Region

Inter-regional macroeconomics is a useful approach to regional analysis, and tells us a great deal about the links between regions in the national economy. On the other hand, it throws virtually no light on what happens *within* regions. In effect, it abstracts from distance; and how can we fully understand the space economy unless we analyse the economic effects of distance? Moreover, it implicitly assumes that regions are homogeneous, a necessary assumption if we wish to treat the parameters of inter-regional multiplier and trade models as having stable and constant values.

Yet the most obvious feature of the space economy is its non-homogeneity. We find that there are agglomerations in economic activity and in population distribution at given locations. These agglomerations are visible regardless of the focus of our inspection: within the national economy some regions have denser populations, higher shares of industrial activity and a more cosmopolitan outlook than others; within the single region there are dominant centres (clusters of people and industry) towards which flows of population, goods and services, communications and traffic gravitate; even within an individual city there is a nucleus or nuclei where most of the city's business, commercial and social activities take place and which stand out if we glance at, say, maps showing the density of intracity traffic flows.

Acceptance of the lack of uniformity in the space economy and recognition that it may have economic significance lead us to the concept of nodal, or polarized regions. Nodal regions are composed of heterogeneous units (e.g. the distribution of human population leads to cities, towns, villages and sparsely inhabited rural areas – in other words, a hierarchy of settlements), but these are closely interrelated with each other functionally. As suggested above, these functional interconnexions are revealed in flow phenomena. These flows do not occur at even rates over space. The heaviest flows tend to polarize towards and from the dominant node (or nodes), usually large cities. Around each node there will be a zone of influence or spatial field in which interaction of many kinds takes place. However, as the force of distance exerts itself the flow densities decline as we move away from the control centre. Eventually, at a certain radius they will fall below a critical level and this sets the outer limits of the spatial field. That these flows vary directly with the size (or attraction) of the node and inversely with distance from it forms the basis of gravity models, the most operational technique for polarization analysis.

Another technique which is useful for the identification of the hierarchical structure of nodes is graph analysis. (See, for example, Nystuen and Dacey (1961) and Boudeville (1966, pp. 28–30, 38–41).) This provides a method enabling us to quantify the degree of association between pairs of population centres so as to identify the networks of strongest association. Association is measured by the direction and magnitude of economic or social flows (for example, telephone calls or personal trip movements for analysis within a region, or inter-regional trade for analysis between regions). The flows can be represented in matrix form. To find the nodes we cancel out all but the strongest flow into or out of each centre. From this we can reduce the hierarchy of nodes to an abstract network of points and lines, for instance, with a binary graph. Two important principles are adhered to: (a) a node is independent when its largest flow is to a smaller centre, subordinate when its largest flow is to a larger centre; (b) transitivity – if X is subordinate to Y and Y subordinate to Z, then X is also subordinate to Z. Application of these principles enables us to order the hierarchy.

The functional linkages within regions can be traced from many sources: the distribution channels of retail and wholesale goods, and the locations from which consumers of centrally located social services, cultural and leisure facilities are drawn; intraregional commodity flows, commuting patterns and migration flows; telephone and other communication densities; labour catchment areas and journey-to-work patterns. Many of these linkages can be summed up in the city–region relationship. However, nodal regions are themselves linked together in a wider spatial framework. Unless all regions are of similar size and experience similar rates of growth, the regional system as a whole will exhibit a degree of imbalance and one or two regions will dominate the others. Even the inter-regional framework is hierarchical. However, polarization flows in the national economy are more frequently related to production links than to the service connexions which dominate intraregional flows. These economy-wide linkages include transportation and communication networks, power grids, oil and gas pipelines, inter-regional migration rates and money flows, and inter-regional trade in raw materials.

Exploration of the nature of nodal regions requires us to explain the unevenness of economic activity over space. This means showing why agglomeration of industry and people is normally more efficient than dispersal. We have consequently to examine the agglomeration aspects of location theory – indivisibilities, that is, internal and external economies of scale, interindustry technological economies and urbanization economies. We have also to show why people find it beneficial and necessary to order themselves into communities of different size, and this calls for an explanation of the origins and development of the urban hierarchy. Furthermore, this hierarchy once developed has a feedback effect on the location of economic activities since many consumer goods industries and most services are market-oriented.

3 Location and Agglomeration[1]

Agglomeration Economies

Agglomeration tendencies in location can be studied at several different levels. The most important of these is to explain why within a region economic activities conglomerate at a few centres rather than form a pattern of even dispersion over the region as a whole. But this is not the only level of inquiry. We also need to show why production and population cluster together in certain regions of the economy, and why because of locational inertia this build-up is self-sustaining so that in the absence of intervention the degree of regional imbalance is intensified. Finally, some attention should be given to the theory of urban location. Urban firms balance their desire for accessibility against high central-site rents and congestion costs, and the result determines whether such a firm will locate at the city centre or at some distance from it. Also, certain types of business establishment will tend to agglomerate together in order that commuter trips may be minimized.

The main agglomeration economies can be classified into several categories, most of which are due to scale effects or indivisibilities.[2] An exception is where firms by agglomerating together (for example, to exploit industrial linkages[3]) gain

1. It is beyond the scope of this book to go into the development of all aspects of location theory. For general discussion see Lösch (1954), Greenhut (1956), Lefeber (1966) and Isard (1956). See also Richardson (1969, chs. 3–5), in particular ch. 4, sections 1–3, for a treatment of the profit-maximizing theory of location in terms of space cost and space revenue curves.

2. This point is urged very strongly by Bos (1965).

3. For example, Hoover (1948, pp. 117–18) includes under this heading economies of locational integration, e.g. the proximity of blast

from savings in transport costs. The agglomeration economies related to scale are: internal economies; economies external to the firm but internal to the industry – Isard calls these localization economies[3]; and external economies to an industry, that is, gains from firms in all industries as a result of increases in total economic size at a given location, which consist primarily of urbanization economies. The influence of internal economies is self-evident; in industries operating under decreasing cost conditions there will tend to be agglomeration within production units subject to constraints imposed by rising freight costs over wide market areas and by external diseconomy effects. To the extent that scale economies act as a barrier to new entrants, their presence will tend to perpetuate existing locations.

Agglomeration advantages for firms in the same industry include gravitation to raw material sources or to non-transportable resource facilities and, given uneven population densities, the need for later firms to locate beside the first producer in an urban centre in order to exploit the high demand potential of such a location. But the main advantages accrue from external scale economies: the ability to support and have access to R and D facilities; the development of a skilled labour pool (in periods of labour shortage, the scope for 'poaching' from rival firms is a locational diseconomy); the growth of auxiliary industries; development of markets for raw materials. These are some of the more obvious examples.

The presence of such economies might explain why an industry stays at a location which is disadvantageous from a cost point of view. Since they are related to scale they are more likely to influence the location of small firms because large

---

furnaces and steelworks, and the production of complementary products by industries at adjacent locations (motor vehicles and components for instance). The technological linkages gained from an industrial complex at a single location discussed by Isard are also relevant here (Isard, Schooler and Vietorisz, 1959).

3. It is this aspect which figured so largely in Weber's analysis of locational agglomeration, see pp. 73–7 below.

firms can create their own scale economies internally. In other words, the boundary between internal economies of large-scale production and economies external to the firm but internal to the industry may be very blurred.

The strongest agglomeration advantages are economies external to individual industries. Since such economies are probably greatest in urban centres, they are often referred to as *urbanization economies* (Isard, 1956, pp. 182–8), or *economies of urban concentration* (Hoover, 1948). They include access to a larger market; the development of urban labour markets and pools of managerial talent; the presence of commercial,[1] banking and financial facilities (including cheaper capital); economies connected with transport services (e.g. improved terminal facilities); communication economies (i.e. opportunities for face-to-face contact with specialist services such as accountants, business consultants and advertising firms); the existence of social, cultural and leisure facilities which influence location decisions; and economies of scale in public services, particularly reductions in the unit costs of energy with increased demand. Another influence is the growth pole concept stressed by Perroux, Hirschman and others according to which rapid economic growth requires a concentration of diverse, though interrelated, activities in a few large centres. For reasons of this kind, for many firms the advantages of urban locations are overwhelming and large centres offer external economies not found in smaller units. On the other hand, large concentrations incur pecuniary diseconomies such as rising land values, wage costs and traffic congestion costs. These diseconomies rarely destroy the pull of urban locations, but they often lead to agglomeration at suburban rather than at core sites.

Not all external economies and diseconomies are related to scale. Chinitz (1961) has reacted against the influence of scale by attempting to relate these economies to market organization and industry structure. He suggests a number of tentative hypotheses: that oligopolistic environments have lower en-

1. For example, the concentration of wholesaling facilities in urban centres reduces the level of inventories firms need to hold.

trepreneurial birth rates and are less receptive to an in-migration of entrepreneurs than competitive ones; small firms have a much greater chance of obtaining loans in their home locality, but if the industrial organization there is competitive rather than oligopolistic, their ability to borrow money is enhanced; if there is a dominant industry in an area, its wage levels influence other industries; since large firms create so many of their auxiliary services internally, they may not be available externally in oligopolistic environments with the consequence that new firms must start big. In other words external economies are greater in areas where industrial structures are competitive.

Weber and Locational Agglomeration

Weber's analysis deserves some consideration since he was the first location theorist to treat agglomeration explicitly. (See Friedrich, 1929.)[1] He discussed agglomeration mainly in terms of what Hoover calls *localization economies*, that is, economies of scale which are external to the firm but internal to the industry.

To understand his analysis we must first define two crucial Weberian concepts, *locational weight* and *critical isodapane*. The locational weight is the total weight of all goods (products, materials, fuel, etc.) that have to be transported to and from the production site per unit of output. It consists of the weight of a unit of the finished product plus the weight of localized materials (that is materials which are *not* available at all sites) required per unit of output. An isodapane is a curve of equal transport costs. If we take the minimum transport cost (M.T.C.) site (P_1) and plot around this point all the loci for a given level of transport costs higher than at P_1 we obtain, assuming transportation is possible in all directions, a closed curve – the isodapane. We have a series of such isodapanes for

1. In fact, Weber's location theory stressed two primary locational forces, transport orientation and labour orientation. Location was decided by agglomerating tendencies only when neither transport cost savings nor labour cost differentials were dominant.

all values of transport cost higher than the minimum at P_1; for high transport cost values these curves will approximate to circles.

Isodapanes measure deviations from the M.T.C. point. If one of the isodapanes exceeds the M.T.C. point by an amount equal to the non-transport cost economies obtainable at an alternative site, then this curve is the critical isodapane in relation to this alternative. If this site lies within the critical isodapane, then it is a more efficient production location than the M.T.C. point.

An understanding of these two concepts enables us to describe the Weberian theory of agglomeration. Let us consider two plants, a large one and a small one, located respectively at their M.T.C. sites. Their outputs are Q and q respectively. It will pay the smaller plant to move adjacent to the large one if the resulting gains from agglomeration are larger than the increase in transport costs involved in deviating from its M.T.C. site. Let the increase in agglomeration economies due to the addition of output q to Q be represented by

$$A_{Q+q} - A_Q.$$

Additional transport costs incurred in shifting production from q's original site to that next to Q are equal to $Ldqt$ where L = the locational weight, d = the distance of q from Q, and t = the transport rate.

It is clear that if $A_{Q+q} - A_Q > Ldqt$ agglomeration will take place.

An important question is the maximum distance over which the agglomerating force of a large production centre extends. If we call this maximum distance D, then

$$LDt = (A_{Q+q} - A_Q)/q.$$

We may call $(A_{Q+q} - A_Q)/q$ the agglomeration function $f_A(Q)$. Thus, we may write

$$f_A(Q) = LDt.$$

In other words, the radius, within which the agglomerating force of a production of output Q is effective, is directly proportional to the value of the agglomeration function, while it is inversely proportional to the locational weight L and the transport rate t.

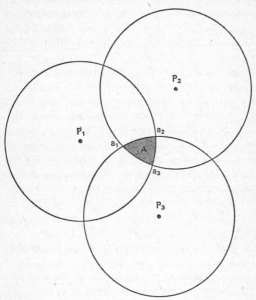

Figure 1

The analysis may also be illustrated diagrammatically. In Figure 1 we have three production units (P_1, P_2 and P_3) each of which is located at its M.T.C. point. If agglomeration economies from locating these three units together can be gained at an alternative site, whether agglomeration is possible depends on whether the critical isodapanes relating to such a site intersect. The three production units shown are close enough together and the agglomeration economies sufficiently large that this condition is satisfied. Agglomeration should therefore take place at a site within the common shaded segment, provided that the combined levels of output can be produced at such a site. However, this is only the beginning of the problem. Every point within the common segment is a *possible* agglomeration site, since production at any of these points is cheaper than at the three scattered M.T.C. locations.

Weber argued that the optimal site will be that which offers the lowest transport cost for the total combined output. In effect, this means that the largest of the three units of production will attract the smaller units to a location within the segment nearer to its original M.T.C. point. Because the largest unit of production will then have changed its position less than the others, then the total deviations from M.T.C. points are minimized.

However, this derivation of the optimal site within the common segment is unsatisfactory. In the first place, agglomeration from several M.T.C. points would only occur if either (i) plants were being started from scratch or (ii) relocation did not involve transition costs. What usually happens is that new plants entering the market will tend to gain localization economies by locating next to established production centres which already offer external economies of scale. Secondly, even within the framework of Weberian theory it is most unlikely that the actual agglomeration site will be the optimal M.T.C. within the common segment. Since all sites within the common segment are preferable to the original scattered M.T.C. sites, and since the cost savings from agglomeration are only obtainable if all plants choose the *same* location, we have a location game situation. Each firm would prefer the point on the segment nearest to its original M.T.C. site (i.e. P_1 prefers a_1, P_2 prefers a_2, and P_3 prefers a_3). The actual agglomeration centre depends on resolution of the conflict of interests of the three plants. This depends on how much each firm is willing to concede, and concessions are determined by bargaining power[1].

1. There are several co-operative procedures: Isard and Smith refer to (i) equal-cost decrement, (ii) equal-cost increment, (iii) action compromise, (iv) equidistant compromise, (v) Zeuthen-type concession, (vi) split-the-difference concession, (vii) distance-decrement concession, and

Reverting to Weber's original analysis, there are three points of general comment. Firstly, Weber's list of agglomeration economies was not comprehensive; in particular, he excluded institutional factors such as economies due to interest, insurance and taxes. Secondly, his analysis is not easily made operational since the agglomeration function is a theoretical construct which is difficult to quantify. As is well known, external economies are notoriously hard to measure. Thirdly, Weber suggested that agglomeration cost savings were greatest in industries with a high value added, and that increasing population density and decreasing transport rates (by extending the critical isodapanes) both increase agglomeration. He thought that these agglomeration tendencies might be built into the economic development process with the result that locational change would be characterized by increasing agglomeration.

Transport Costs and Location

Although high transport costs tend to encourage locational dispersion by giving scattered plants a certain degree of protection, the normal effect of the transportation factor is to induce agglomeration in an industry. Firstly, if the transport costs on raw materials needed to make a unit of finished product differ from those per unit of final output, then (assuming that raw materials are available at one source) the optimal location will, *ceteris paribus*, be at the material source or the market rather than at an intermediate site. Secondly, the attractiveness of end-point locations for all firms will be increased when we take account of terminal costs and economies of longer hauls. Thirdly, where alternative modes of transport are used, there will be an advantage in locating at the break

---

(viii) leader–conceder concession procedures. This is by no means a comprehensive list of feasible solutions in the three-person location game, but it serves to illustrate the indeterminacy of a problem which Weber assumed settled. For definitions of the above procedures and for a full discussion of the solution of location problems by means of game theory see Isard and Smith (1967) and Stevens (1961).

in the transport network (that is the transshipment point). This advantage will be particularly great for processing industries and explains why such industries are very often located near ports and rail terminals. As a consequence of these factors, transport nodes and sites near main traffic routes are potential centres of agglomeration.

Locational Interdependence

By locational interdependence we mean that the location decision of a new plant may be affected by locations chosen and policies pursued by its competitors. This assumes that oligopoly is the typical market structure in the space economy. The relevance of the locational interdependence framework is that it may lead to agglomeration even *in the absence* of internal and external economies of scale, substantial spatial differences in production costs, and marked variations in demand.

The problems of locational interdependence have normally been analysed under very restrictive assumptions: two or three firm models, linear rather than areal markets, and costless and instantaneous relocation. Hotelling (1929) argued that duopolists would agglomerate at the centre of a linear market even though this maximized rather than minimized transport costs because only with agglomeration would there be no incentive for one of the firms to jump over the other and secure a larger share of protected market.[1] This finding is, however, dependent upon his assumptions. If we permit demand to be elastic, or if we replace the finite linear market with a circle or an endless stretch, or if each firm takes account of the possible reactions of its rival, then the results change and agglomeration becomes less likely.

With three firms Lerner and Singer (1939) argued that there would be complete instability in location, but if we accept that each firm will realize that its competitors can relocate then the location position will settle down, probably with one

1. For discussion and criticisms see Lösch (1954, pp. 72–5), Ferguson (1966, pp. 273–6) and Devletoglou (1965).

firm at one quartile of the market and the other two clustered at the other quartile. With more than three producers, plants will be either dispersed or clustered in pairs depending on the prevailing location pattern when new firms enter the market. In all cases the actual distribution will differ from the optimal, though the difference becomes smaller as we increase the number of producers.

The 'hopping over' sequences characteristic of spatial competition theory can be ruled out if we assume that relocation costs are positive and heavy. However, locational interdependence has still to be reckoned with when new firms enter an industry. The relaxation of other assumptions of the spatial competition models in some cases reinforces agglomeration, in others encourages dispersion. The more important influences include:

(i) *Elasticity of demand.* If demand is elastic the need to minimize freight costs is more urgent, and this will tend to result in dispersed locations.

(ii) *Freight rates.* Low transport rates will induce agglomeration, but if they are high the distance over which goods can be sold is limited and dispersion is necessary.

(iii) *Shape of the marginal cost curve.* If marginal costs are rising the addition of freight costs does not have a major effect on the factory price; heavy freight absorption means a relatively wide market area (Greenhut, 1956). The gains from dispersion are more uncertain, and agglomeration is more likely.

(iv) *Cost differentials between sites and non-transportable resources.* If there is a least cost location and higher production costs at other sites exceed transport cost savings gained from tapping nearby market segments, then agglomeration is inevitable. Similarly, the existence of an important non-transportable resource (deep harbour, mineral deposits, etc.) can have a strong agglomerating effect on certain industries.

(v) *Uncertainty.* A site adjacent to existing plants usually involves fewer risks than a new untested distant location.

(vi) *Uneven population distribution.* The seminal analyses of spatial competition all assumed uniform population distribution. In reality, high density population centres will induce agglomeration because of their demand potential appeal.

(vii) *Personal contacts.* The existence of personal contacts between producers and their suppliers, customers and financiers lessen the need to pay attention to rivals' locations. Whether this results in concentration or dispersion depends on circumstances.

(viii) *Pricing systems.* Pricing systems other than f.o.b. net mill pricing, such as uniform delivered prices or single basing point prices, usually involve spatial price discrimination against near consumers. They consequently strengthen agglomeration tendencies by reducing the importance of distance.

The interdependence of location decisions may induce agglomeration by making it easier for each firm to keep pace with its rivals' policies and by reducing risks. If we introduce realistic conditions, agglomeration tendencies are on the whole strengthened.

Location Decision Criteria

Industry tends to agglomerate in a few prosperous regions of an economy, and this process is usually self-sustaining. In the last century basic industry was strongly attracted to sources of raw materials and fuel supplies, but the coming of electric power and changing technology greatly widened the locational choice. The build-up of industry near large high-income population centres indicated an increasing trend towards market orientation.

There has been considerable evidence over the last twenty years that a high proportion of industry is 'footloose', that is, capable of being located anywhere (perhaps about 70 per cent of manufacturing industry). (See, for example, Nicholson (1956) and Luttrell (1962).) If this is the case, we might have expected more locational shifts out of the prosperous regions as labour shortages and other congestion costs develop. Although locational shifts have taken place on a fairly substantial scale, these have occurred in an environment where inducements were given to persuade firms to move and where expansion at home sites was in many cases prohibited. There has still been considerable locational inertia as far as inter-regional transfers are concerned. Why has this been so?

One factor has been that locations no longer possessing direct cost advantages have nevertheless continued to be preferred because they offer large external economies. Apart from this, the most plausible explanation of locational inertia, market orientation and agglomeration in certain regions is that the location decision is determined by criteria other than profit maximization. The profit-maximization assumption is in many ways not very appropriate to location theory. It leads to models with low predictive power. In the first place, the strong market orientation of modern industry, even in sectors where spatial cost differentials are large, is more consistent, as we shall see, with revenue than with profit maximization. Secondly, it is an observable fact of life that individuals including business executives prefer to live in some areas rather than in others. They receive 'psychic income' from expressing their space preferences, and the difficulty of assigning monetary values to psychic income makes it almost impossible to allow for this phenomenon in a profit-maximizing model. Moreover, it is well known that profit maximization becomes more difficult to handle in (a) conditions of great uncertainty and (b) dynamic analysis.[1] Location decisions are obviously taken only at very infrequent intervals and have repercussions over a long period of time. Because of the unpredictability of future changes in spatial costs and prices and the difficulties of measuring external economies, which figure so largely in location decisions, it is improbable that firms will go to extreme lengths to find the most profitable location. Relocation costs of existing plants are very heavy, and can only be recovered over a long period; if the long-term advantages of a new site are uncertain this makes for locational inertia. Finally, since time preference and risk premiums[2] vary from

1. It is arguable, however, that since profits accrue over time and are certainly obtained in a time period later than the period of production, profit theory cannot be analysed in purely static terms.
2. Risks are much heavier at new than at old-established locations.

firm to firm, the profit-maximizing location for one plant of a given scale will not necessarily maximize profits for another plant of the same size. Thus, profit maximization is no more an objective or determinate criterion than one based on non-maximizing assumptions.

In the U.K. most manufacturing plants serve a national market rather than purely regional markets. In a British context, market orientation usually means no more than a preference for locating in the more populous higher-income regions of the South-East and Midlands, and market access advantages are to be explained more by reference to personal contacts and accessibility to customers than by savings in transport costs. To the extent that market orientation is a feature of free location decisions by modern industry it is more consistent with revenue than with profit maximization hypotheses. Of course, in the special case where cost differentials do not exist, then for a given output revenue maximization is equal to profit maximization; but where there are spatial cost variations the optimal location will differ.

Applying revenue maximization in a spaceless economy, the firm will produce the level of output corresponding to the peak of the total revenue curve where marginal revenue is zero, though this may be subject to a profit constraint so that total costs have to be identified as well. In the space economy, both location and output are variables and in taking a location decision firms will lack the experience of operation which simplifies estimation of total costs and revenues. Moreover, since location decisions are made for long periods long-run sales maximization is more relevant than short-run. This calls for estimation of *future* costs and revenues for plants larger than the one initially established (most new plants build up from a low level rather than begin operation at their maximum feasible output).

These additional complications mean that revenue maximizing location decisions are normally taken in *ad hoc* fashion rather than in the light of precise calculations of total costs and revenues. The main criteria are: (a) a site offering the maximum long-run growth of sales at a reasonable profit, and

(b) a site with scope for plant extension. The first criterion rules out isolated locations regardless of any cost advantages. On the other hand, the existence of a profit constraint often makes firms wary of locating near city centres where site costs and congestion costs are heavy. For similar reasons, room for plant expansion also constrains the choice of the sales maximizing location. This is not inconsistent with the revenue-maximizing hypothesis, but simply means a long-run rather than a short-run time horizon.

We have argued that a reluctance to seek new locations in underdeveloped or formerly depressed regions results in a continued build-up of activities in a limited number of regions. This situation prevails even in cases where the untested locations offer substantial potential cost advantages and where existing locations suffer from labour shortages and congestion costs.

Firms very rarely look for a new site unless their present one offers no room for expansion or has some other major defect which rules out profitable production and/or growth. When plants have to be moved, no great efforts are made to seek the most profitable location. If comparative cost studies are carried out only one or two sites are compared. Speed and ease of decision are often major influences in determining which site is selected. Moreover, the appearance of an area, the quality of social life, the availability of leisure facilities and other environmental preferences may be more critical in site selection than production cost advantages. Also, among location advantages non-measurable factors, such as the tenor of local management–labour relations and the attitude of workers towards technical change, may be given greater weight than quantifiable ones (e.g. labour cost differentials, transport cost savings). When new plants are set up, the founders normally prefer to start business where they live rather than seek the most profitable site either in their own or in other regions. Finally, locational inertia remains in many cases even in the face of substantial financial inducements to relocate and controls on expansion at existing sites. These empirical generalizations suggest that maximizing assumptions may not be the most appropriate for location theory. (For evidence, though scanty, see Luttrell (1962), Cameron and Reid (1966), Greenhut (1956) and Loasby (1967).)

Business firms may choose more limited objectives than profit (or revenue) maximization in their location decision or when considering whether or not to relocate. They may set themselves minimal standards of achievement which they anticipate will ensure long-run viability and bring about a reasonable level of profits. This type of behaviour can be described as 'satisficing'. Its implications are: firms will avoid risky locations especially in regions without experience of their particular industry, and they will usually prefer the security of centres of agglomeration; on the other hand, they will be chary of sites involving rising congestion costs even if they have high market potential.

Satisficing behaviour does not require firms to make precise calculations since potential locations suggest themselves, being found near transport routes and/or raw material sources or labour pools and/or nodal points and major population centres. Once the highly congested core sites have been ruled out, the choice from among several possible locations may be decided by environmental preferences or on other personal grounds. Although satisficing hypotheses yield some indeterminacy in location they have the advantage of being able to take account of psychic income. They therefore help to explain why firms may still freely choose locations in one or two regions even if other areas offer more profitable locations.

Location within Urban Centres

Agglomeration of plants and establishments can also be observed within urban centres, for economic activities are not regularly dispersed over the area of a city or town. In a centralized city (i.e. a city with a single core) a firm engaged in consumer goods production or in the service trades will have to balance, when choosing a location, the market potential and accessibility advantages of being close to the centre against higher site costs (rent).

Alonso (1964) has dealt with this problem by adopting the concept of *bid rent functions*. These are hypothetical iso-profit curves which show how the rent of land must vary with distance for the firm to obtain the same profits regardless of location. The firm will locate at that site where the actual rent of land is equal to the rent the firm is prepared to pay to assure itself the highest possible profits. If we assume that the actual rent of land at each location is given, and we ignore size-of-site constraints, the firm will locate where the actual rent function is tangential to the *lowest possible* bid rent curve.[1]

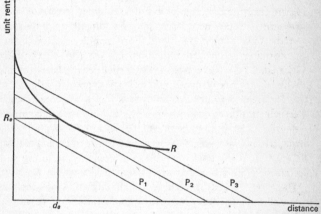

Figure 2

Bid rent curves slope downwards for, since revenue declines and operating costs (including transport costs) increase with distance, bid rents must fall with distance for profits to remain constant.

In Figure 2 the rent function R is drawn in a way which assumes that land rent declines with increasing distance from the city centre. The equilibrium location is at d_e where the rent function is tangential to the bid rent curve, P_2. If the actual

1. Since profits are a residual after payment of operating and site costs, the lower the price of land the higher the profits.

rent function had been more concave from the origin than the bid rent curves, we would have obtained an end-point solution (i.e. location at the city centre). The bid rent curves of establishments for which a central location is essential (e.g. retail outlets catering for large numbers of customers or business equipment and stationery firms which need to be close to offices and commercial establishments) will have steep slopes.

In this model, site rent (which reflects the limited supply of land available in a city centre and the demand for sites) distributes economic activities spatially according to their need for accessibility. There will be an agglomeration of establishments near the core, but these will be confined to certain kinds of activity which need to have access (directly or indirectly) to the maximum populations. For example, establishments performing specialized functions will tend to be centrally located. But other establishments, such as industrial plants with heavy space demands, will seek a peripheral location.

The main defect of this analysis is that it assumes a single nucleus within a city, whereas it has long been recognized that in a large city there will be several focal points (or nuclei) each of which could serve as a centre of agglomeration for firms. These nuclei may form a hierarchy, resulting in a hierarchically structured set of rent peaks within the city. These rent peaks have the effect of attracting or repelling establishments, again inducing agglomerations of particular types of activity.

However, there are other complicating influences. For example, one nucleus may develop around a transshipment zone and this will tend to attract heavy manufacturing, warehousing and wholesaling. Similarly, hotels, theatres and shops catering primarily for non-residents may cluster near passenger transport terminals, while other establishments with accessibility requirements (banks, offices, newspapers and shops) will agglomerate near the main routes of intracity transit.

Agglomeration of similar establishments also offers certain external economies (e.g. the advantages of having an office and general commercial zone, the commuting cost savings from having shops close to each other), while some dissimilar activities will agglomerate because they are complementary (offices and snack bars, theatres and restaurants, hospitals and flower stalls). These agglomeration patterns may also show a hierarchical structure in that a large city may have a secondary office zone and several suburban shopping centres.

Another element to be considered is the repulsion between certain kinds of activity, of which the separation of high-class residences from heavy-industry zones is the most obvious example.

Thus, agglomerative and deglomerative forces within the city reflect far more than the desire for accessibility and the effects of high rents at central sites.

4 The Nodal Hierarchy

Central Place Theory

A major feature of nodal regions is that urban population, far from being distributed equally among centres of similar size, is distributed among centres of different size which together form themselves into an urban hierarchy. The main reason for its development is that it is more efficient to supply some goods and services in small centres but to supply others in larger centres. Once the hierarchy has evolved, however, we find evidence of dominance by the larger centres and of the polarized flows of economic phenomena which characterize nodal regions. It follows that explaining the evolution of the urban hierarchy is a vital element in understanding nodal regions. The core of this explanation is to be found in central place theory. (See Christaller (1966), Lösch (1954), Berry and Garrison (1958), Berry (1967) and Dacey (1966).)

According to this theory, an urban centre's main functions are to act as a service centre for its hinterland (*complementary region*), supplying it with central goods and services such as retail services, commercial, banking and professional services, educational, leisure and cultural facilities and urban government services. These services can be ranked into higher and lower orders depending on the demand *threshold* (i.e. the minimum viable level required to support the service) and the *range* (i.e. the outer limits of the market area for each service). These two factors determine the number and size of central places supplying each service, and hence a central place hierarchy develops. Small central places and their complementary regions will be included within the market areas of larger centres. In long-run equilibrium, when the whole area of the system is covered, the service areas will be hexagonal in shape and space will be covered by several honeycomb lattices with hexagons of different size superimposed upon each other.[1]

Provided there is an upper and a lower limit (i.e. range and threshold) to the market area of each service, a hierarchy emerges. This can be shown as follows.

Assume an area supplied with n types of central good, ranked in ascending order from 1 to n. The central place supplying n will need the largest market area. As many of these centres (let us call them A-centres) will exist as there are threshold sales levels for good n, and the central places will tend to be sited at the centre of the market area. All other central goods and services $(n-1, n-2, \ldots, 1)$ will also be supplied by A-centres.

However, there will be some service $(n-i)$ where population and income located in the gaps between the threshold market areas of A-centres supplying $n-i$ are great enough to justify further threshold market areas within these gaps. These gaps can be more efficiently supplied by a second order of centres (B-centres), hence new central places of smaller size emerge. The central service $n-i$ is called the *hierarchical marginal service*, and the number of these marginal services determines the number of orders of central place in the hierarchy. B-centres will, of course, also supply all lower central goods and services. Similarly, if $n-j$ is also a hierarchical marginal service (where $j>i$), a third set of central places (C-centres) will grow up.

If there are M hierarchical marginal services there will be M sets of central places (A, B, C, ..., M). The result is a central place hierarchy, pyramidal in the sense that the number of centres in each order will be inversely related to the size-class of the order. There will also tend to be some relationship between size-class and distance, since higher order centres will be wider apart than lower order centres.

A more specific illustration of the role of central services as a determinant of the urban hierarchy is the supply of urban

1. The emergence of hexagonal market areas is not critical to a central place hierarchy model as is shown by Mills and Lav (1964).

government services. Economies of scale vary for urban government services of different types so that some services can be supplied (and possibly financed) more efficiently in small urban units while others require large units.[1] However, even where technical factors favour large urban units the desire for community participation and other non-economic factors may make the favoured size of urban unit less than the technical optimum.

Nevertheless, a multilevel administrative and fiscal system probably provides public services more cheaply than a single unit system, though there are clearly severe limits on the divisibility into hierarchy orders. *Ceteris paribus*, large units have advantages other than scale economies: they minimize areal spillovers in costs and benefits, they have superior revenue-raising powers, and they have the political advantage of eliminating the need for *open* cross-community subsidies. To the extent that the devolution of functions from central to urban governments strengthens the position of large units in a multilevel hierarchy, they reinforce polarization and nodal tendencies.

Central place theory is relevant to urban and regional planning because a hierarchical system provides an efficient means of administering and allocating resources to regions. Major central places are often the key points of growth in their region and determine the rate of economic development over the region as a whole. It is clear, therefore, that the spatial and size distribution of urban centres is a vital element in the structure of nodal regions and gives rise to the concepts of dominance and polarization which characterize this structure. Central place theory presents the most obvious model for explaining the growth of the urban hierarchy, and also as a by-product stresses the interdependence between urban centres and their surrounding regions.

1. For an analysis of this complex question see Brazer (1959), Hirsch (1959) and Gupta and Hutton (1968). Examples of functions carried out more efficiently by large units include public housebuilding (especially if industrialized building techniques can be adopted), main engineering services, water supply and local government administration.

On the other hand, it does not offer a complete explanation of urban growth. As large cities grow some services are supplied which have nothing to do with catering for a market area hinterland; for example, services may be transferred from households or business units to specialized service establishments, while metropolitan living may generate its own needs such as car-parking facilities and social welfare agencies. Moreover, in densely populated regions large centres may develop in close proximity to each other leading to social and commercial interaction, and specialization of function of the kind not explicable in terms of central place analysis. Similarly, the development of both residential and industrial suburbs lies outside the central place framework. Also large towns and cities often expand as manufacturing locations because they offer flexible labour markets and agglomeration economies generally. Where their manufacturing plants cater for national more than for regional markets, the growth of urban centres may be predicted more precisely by urban base than by central place models.

The Central Place Hierarchy and the Rank–Size Rule

The hierarchical structure of nodal centres will be reflected not only in their spatial ordering but in their relative size. The system of urban centres may be categorized vertically according to which centres are ranked by population size, yielding an urban size hierarchy.

The most well-known attempt to represent this hierarchy is the *rank–size rule*, referred to by Singer, Zipf and others. This states that in an urban system the population of a given city tends to be equal to the population of the largest city divided by the rank of city-size into which the given city falls. In practice, the basic formula may be modified by a constant to yield a better fit to the distribution. Thus

$$M^a P_M = P_A = Q,$$

where a and Q are constants, P_M and P_A represent the populations of the Mth and the largest city respectively, and M is the size and rank of Mth city.

The rank–size rule implies a general theory of urban systems. Beckmann (1958) has suggested that there is a strong correspondence between the central place hierarchy and the rank–size rule.[1] The analysis depends upon the assumption of a stable relationship between the population of a central place and the population of the market area served by it (which except in the case of the lowest ranking central place will include the populations of smaller central places). It may be summarized as follows:

Let M = order of place, P_M = population served by place of order M, C_M = population of place of rank M, K = proportion of population served located in the central place, n = number of places in order $M-1$ served by places in order M, and R_1 = rural population served by place of lowest rank. The population served by the smallest centre[2]

$$P_1 = \frac{R_1}{1-K}$$

We may also express the population of centre M and the population served by it respectively as:

$$C_M = KP_M \qquad\qquad 41$$

and
$$P_M = C_M + nP_{M-1}. \qquad\qquad 42$$

Therefore
$$P_M = \frac{n}{1-K}P_{M-1}. \qquad\qquad 43$$

However, it is clear that
$$P_{M-1} = \frac{n}{1-K}P_{M-2}$$

1. For a dissenting view see Dacey (1966).
2. The derivation is simple:

$$P_1 = C_1 + R_1$$
$$C_1 = KP_1.$$

Therefore
$$P_1 = KP_1 + R_1$$
$$P_1 = \frac{R_1}{1-K}.$$

while $\quad P_{M-2} = \dfrac{n}{1-K} P_{M-3}, \quad$ etc.

so that $\quad P_M = \left(\dfrac{n}{1-K}\right)^{M-1} P_1.$ \hfill 44

Substituting $\dfrac{R_1}{1-K}$ for P_1 we obtain

$$P_M = \left(\frac{n}{1-K}\right)^{M-1} \times \frac{R_1}{1-K} = \frac{R_1\, n^{M-1}}{(1-K)^M} \hfill 45$$

while $\qquad\qquad C_M = \dfrac{KR_1 n^{M-1}}{(1-K)^M}.$ \hfill 46

The smallest central place has a population equal to $KR_1/(1-K)$ while each order place has a population equal to $n/(1-K) \times$ the population of the place of the next order. The more orders in the system the closer city sizes will conform to a continuous distribution. Most important of all, if K is small relative to 1, then from $n/(1-K)$ we know that the product of the rank of a place and its population size will approximate to a constant. However K may not be small especially in the heavily urbanized economy, and this will lead to distortions of the rank–size rule.

Moreover, as equations 45 and 46 show, both place size and market-area population increase exponentially as the level of hierarchy increases. This is consistent with the empirical hypothesis that the number of types of business in a centre increases with the level of centre.

Tinbergen (1961) argued that industries could be ranked according to their number of production units; that in each centre with an industry of a given rank all industries of lower rank are also located, and that only one production unit of the highest ranking industry is found in a centre. (See also Bos (1965).) This requires that firms in the same industry should be dispersed among centres, whereas as we observed in the last chapter resource-orientation and agglomeration economies may lead to clustering. It is for this reason that central place theory and this analysis is much more relevant to the spatial distribution of retail and service activities and its consequences than to manufacturing.

Similarly, the rank–size rule is less likely to hold in a small densely populated, highly industrial country than in a large economically developed but not too densely populated land mass where most cities in the hierarchy perform regional or sub-regional functions (e.g. the United States).[1]

The Changing Urban Hierarchy in England

Some research has been done on changes in the urban hierarchy.[2] Unfortunately, since the studies refer only to England (or England and Wales), they do not permit us to test how far the central place system in the U.K. conforms to the predicted theoretical pattern and how great is the deviation from the rank–size rule. Nevertheless, they throw valuable light on the spatial structure of urban settlements in a modern economy.

Smith (1968) classified central places in England on the basis of 1965 data and compared the results with Smailes' earlier classification (1938). Such a comparison is imperfect because Smith used a wider range of indicators[3] and a larger number of orders. London, was, of course, in a class by itself (first order). The 606 other main centres listed by Smailes

1. Not that United States data yield a perfect fit. For an early study see Singer (1936). Reference should also be made to Berry (1964).

2. The most comprehensive studies are by Smailes (1944) and by Smith (1968), but also useful are Green (1950 and 1966) and Carruthers (1967).

3. These indicators included: numbers of banks and accountant firms; cinemas, theatres and orchestra; frequency of general market, existence of Marks and Spencers, Woolworths, British Home Stores, Boots Chemists and quality of shopping centre; railway station and depots; class of best hotel and number of A.A. hotels and garages; grammar and comprehensive schools, further education facilities including universities; local weekly morning and evening newspapers; hospitals; post offices; telephone group centre and Area H.Q.; T.V. studio; Football League club; Chamber of Commerce, Stock Exchange, Bank of England branch, and D.E.P. office; total employment.

down to the sub-town category and how they were classified by Smith are summarized below.

Table 7

	Major cities	City	Major town	Town	Sub-town		1965
2A	3						3
2B	5						5
2C	5	1					6
3A	1	19	9				29
3B			46	1			47
3C			32	19	1		52
4A			5	77	3		85
4B				150	30		180
4C				37	127		164
5A				2	32		34
Ungraded					1		1
1938	14	20	92	286	194		606
Equivalent 1965 rank[1]	14	29	99	265	164	35	

The most striking feature is the stability of rankings. The second-order centres remained unchanged 1938–65 apart from the promotion of Coventry and relegation of Bradford.[2] Of the 606 centres, 138 enjoyed a rise in status while 78 declined; a net rise is of course to be expected in a period of over-all population growth. To the extent that there was change, a surprising finding is that promotions to higher ranked centres (3A) mainly occurred in Northern areas (Blackpool, Bolton, Chester, Doncaster, Huddersfield and Lincoln) which though not depressed were less buoyant compared with the South-East and Midlands. This suggests that the

1. The equivalent 1965 rank orders consist of the following categories: 2A, 2B, 2C; 3A; 3B, 3C; 4A, 4B, 4C; 5A, ungraded.
2. The leading 1965 centres (in descending order of importance) were: Manchester, Birmingham and Liverpool (equal), Leeds, Newcastle, Sheffield, Bristol, Nottingham, Leicester, Hull, Southampton, Plymouth, Coventry and Norwich.

relationship between shifts in the central place system and regional development is complex.

On *a priori* grounds we might predict that major promotions in status would be found in prosperous, rapidly developing regions. However, this is too simplified. In the South the influence of London is so strong that major new centres find it difficult to emerge.[1] Rapidly expanding regions tend to absorb their rising population by creating new *small* centres. In the older regions with relatively static populations, gains accrue only to fairly large centres. Extensive gains of this kind are compatible with slower regional growth if this is associated, as is often the case, with a decline of small towns. Moreover, congestion and obsolescence in large cities in such regions may lead to expansion in rather smaller urban places. But the main area of relegation of centres was also in the North – the East Pennine belt from Bradford south through Derbyshire to the Leicester coalfield. Whether the poor environment of much of the area is a consequence or a cause of these changes it is difficult to say. On the other hand, a region of concentrated population growth such as the West Midlands may experience little change in central place status – in this case probably explained by the continued dominance of the redeveloped city centre of Birmingham, the growth of Coventry and the strength of Wolverhampton.

As pointed out above, the fact that England forms only part of a central place system rules out any test of the rank–size rule. It has been suggested that for such a test not only the United Kingdom but Western Europe as a whole forms a complete system. Another prerequisite of a rank–size rule test for Britain would be to correct for the disproportionate size of the metropolis relative to the next largest cities. However, a study confined to England can be used to examine another aspect of the central place system: the relationship between each central place order and inter-urban distance. The metropolis repels second-order centres; the nearest is 77 miles away

1. Exceptions are Guildford, Reading and Southend, while Luton, Swindon and Watford may be expected to improve their rank in the near future.

and the average distance between London and the fourteen next important centres is 151 miles. Within the second order, however, inter-urban distances can be much lower even for high-ranking central places. Thus, Manchester and Liverpool are only 35 miles apart, Leeds and Sheffield 33 miles, Leicester and Nottingham 25 miles, and Birmingham and Coventry only 18 miles.[1] The minimum distance between third-order centres can be smaller, but rarely falls below 12 miles.

The proximity of some of the second-order centres suggests that in highly urbanized regions we have to modify the inference from central place theory of distinct and separate market areas for places of similar size; there are obvious signs of overlapping with zones common to two centres. This problem obviously requires much more detailed investigation than can be attempted here.

Gravity Models

The importance of nodality in regional economics is that it emphasizes the dominance of one (or more) points in space over others and shows how this influence is reduced by distance. The gravity model is an operationally useful tool for assessing nodality. In its most generalized form, the gravity concept can be expressed as:

$$I_{ij} = \frac{KA_i^a \, A_j^b}{d_{ij}^c}, \qquad 47$$

where I_{ij} = expected degree of interaction between centre i and centre j,
A_i, A_j = size or attraction of centres i and j,
d_{ij} = a measure of distance between i and j,
K = a constant
and a, b, c = exponential parameters.

This suggests that interaction between i and j (or the

1. Some centres are relatively isolated, however. Plymouth, Norwich and to a lesser extent Newcastle are examples. The average *minimum* distance between second order centres was 53 miles.

influence of *j* upon *i*) is directly related to the size of *i* and *j* and inversely related to the distance between them. There are various modifications which can be made to this model (for instance, if *i* was merely a point in space we might ignore A_i altogether) but they do not alter it in substance. Sometimes we require to estimate the total interaction of a centre with all other centres, or what is called *potential at i*, P_i.

If

$$P_i = \sum_{j=1} \frac{I_{ij}}{A_i^a}$$

then

$$P_i = K \sum_{j=1} \frac{A_j^b}{d_{ij}^c}.$$

Although various uses have been suggested for models of this kind, the vast majority of applications has related to forecasts of retail trends or inter-city travel patterns.[1] Our argument is that the scope of gravity analysis is much wider provided that the problems of measures of *A*, *d* and the exponents are handled carefully. Indeed, it is not fanciful to suggest that gravity models provide a universal approach for interpreting nodal regions. It should be stressed, however, that gravity models are not deterministic. They do not optimize, but instead predict what is likely to happen. They are concerned with *expected* interaction, and have an obvious link with probability theory. This means that gravity models represent a behavioural rather than an optimizing theory (A. J. Wilson, 1967). We consider this a virtue rather than a vice. On the other hand, a consequence of its dependence on probability theory is that the gravity model works best when applied to broad aggregates composed of a great many individual units. The greater the disaggregation the less reliable the model's predictions.[2]

1. For example see Lakshmanan and Hansen (1965), Lewis and Traill (1968), Zipf (1946), Hammer and Iklé (1957).
2. Another limitation of gravity models is that like most predictive models they forecast on the basis of past behaviour. In cases where new regions or new centres of agglomeration are being opened up and

The units chosen for measurement of size or attraction (A) and distance (d) depend on the problem under consideration, but the choice is large and varied. For studies estimating the influence over space of population centres, population will be used to measure A, and this will sometimes be weighted by income. In retail shopping analyses there are many possible indicators: number of shops (weighted or unweighted), retail sales or employment, area of shopping space, etc. In inter-regional gravity models, gross regional product, regional employment or net manufacturing output may be used. In migration studies employing the gravity concept, attention may be expressed in terms of employment opportunities or *per capita* income. Moreover, if A is quantified in terms of a simple indicator such as population, we may apply different weights for dealing with separate phenomena; such weights might include income, age composition, occupational distribution, proportion of urban residents, capital per head, etc. Distance may be measured in terms of minimum mileage, travel time, transport costs or 'social distance' (e.g. the number of intervening opportunities as in Stouffer's theory of migration, 1940). Again, selection of the distance measure will vary according to the problem studied. In many cases, more sophisticated measures than minimum geographical distance will yield more precise results. For example, in urban traffic studies we will often need to take account of the 'modal split', and use linked gravity models estimating distance separately for car and non-car owners.

Determination of the exponents for the size and distance variables is another serious problem. Many studies have ignored the exponents, thereby implicitly assuming that they have a value of unity. In regard to the exponent to be fitted to the distance variable, J. Q. Stewart argued that it should be 1 or 2, and the law of retail gravitation associated with one of

---

developed, they are of little value. Thus, in retail shopping studies, gravity concepts may be useful for assessing the effect of population growth on existing shopping centres but are unproductive for estimating sales at a new shopping centre, the growth of which requires customers to break away from past patterns of behaviour.

the early pioneers of gravity models (W. J. Reilly) uses an exponent of 2. Hammer and Iklé (1957) used exponents in the range 1·3–1·8 in their telephone and airline traffic research, Carroll and Bevis (1957) fitted an exponent of 1·63 for travel trips in Detroit, while Isard and Peck applied an exponent of 1·7 in a study of inter-regional rail shipments. There are no strong theoretical grounds for an exponent of unity, and indeed the exponents should alter according to the institutional environment and the nature and shape of the distance function chosen. Moreover, there is no practical justification for assuming that the exponent is equal to one, since the technical problem of estimating its value is easily solved by representing d_{ij}^{c} as $c \log d_{ij}$, and estimating c by fitting a linear regression by the least squares method.

It is even less common to apply an exponent to A. Yet we would argue that only by doing so can the gravity model be generalized to explore the real forces at work in nodal regions. As we have seen, nodality reflects the presence of agglomeration economies at certain points, and these economies are primarily related to scale. Similarly, the attraction of a centre is constrained by the emergence of scale diseconomies such as congestion costs.[1] The influence of these external economies and diseconomies can be shown by applying exponents to A greater than one and less than one respectively. However, if agglomeration economies are mainly due to scale, a different exponent will be required for As of different size (i.e. $a \neq b$). Even though it is difficult to identify the impact of *particular* kinds of external economies, their over-all effect may be quantified from the regression coefficients. Using the simple gravity models without exponents does not really avoid the problem, but merely involves the implicit assumption that $a = b = c = 1$.

Gravity models are sometimes criticized as having merely descriptive value and lacking a theoretical framework. While this objection may carry weight against simple population potential indices, it is unconvincing as far as the more complex

1. If d is measured in terms of transport costs and/or travel time, then congestion costs will also be reflected in d.

gravity models are concerned. Where weights and exponents are fitted to the A-variable, and where distance is measured in economic and social rather than in mileage terms, then the gravity approach enables us to test theories which relate to the uneven dispersion of economic activity in response to the pull of agglomerative forces at certain sites, and to a general desire by individuals for accessibility reflected in the minimization of space friction costs.

The scope for application of gravity models is much wider than the obvious examples of retail shopping, intra- and inter-city travel and migration trends. Harris (1954) and Dunn (1956) made pioneering but unsatisfactory attempts to use the gravity concept (or strictly speaking market potential analysis) to explain the location of industry. More recently, Sargent (1968) has suggested that a gravity model may be constructed to express 'journey to work' desires which could be useful in the planning of new towns and new locations for industry. There is considerable scope for gravity techniques in both intraregional and inter-regional analysis. For example, in the first case we might be able to employ gravity models to identify the dominant nodes in a highly complex urban region. In the second, if peripheral regions, as seems plausible, participate less in inter-regional trade than more central regions then gravity concepts may be used in a simulation model of inter-regional trade. In such a model the transport cost–distance parameter will need to be varied for different goods, reflecting the fact that low-value commodities are supplied over shorter distances.[1]

Most gravity studies have been carried out in the United States, but in recent years gravity models have also been used for planning purposes in the United Kingdom. One example is the retail trade forecasting model developed for the East Midlands Planning Council by Pullen.[2] Its objective was to predict retail sales and their distribution in the East Midlands

1. The nearest approaches to a model of this kind have been Leontief and Strout (1963) and A. J. Wilson (1968).
2. I am grateful to Michael Pullen now of Keele University for allowing me to see his research design.

in 1981.[1] A simple distance function had to be adopted because of computer storage constraints. The one selected related minimum distance to average travel time using a bus–car modal split.[2] Also, an exponential distance function was preferred to a simple power function.[3] The reason for this is that an exponential function results in a greater dispersion of sales around a retail centre, and this is more appropriate in highly urbanized regions where we need to take account of shopping trips between neighbouring urban centres of similar size. An inevitable drawback of the forecasting exercise was that size and distance measures referred to the base year. However, these were modified by estimates of changes in the regional distribution of population and employment growth, and by anticipated changes in the bus–car modal split.

Growth Points

The growth point concept represents a link between the naturally evolved structure of nodal regions and physical and regional planning. As we have seen, agglomeration economies make concentrations of production more efficient than dispersal while the balance between scale economies in the supply of central services and the desire for accessibility results in population concentrations arranged in a hierarchy. Growth point analysis can be a useful guide to regional planning if we accept the assumption that the agglomeration resulting from the operation of market forces also brings social benefits. The focus on sub-regional centres for growth helps to bridge the gap between location theory and regional economics. It also helps to impart an element of unity and direction to regional

1. Because retail trade in a region is influenced by shopping behaviour outside its boundaries, the base year (1961) estimates for the region had to be supplemented by sales estimates for the surrounding area (i.e. for two concentric rings each fifteen miles in depth). Experience suggests that a fifteen-mile cut-off point covers 95 per cent of shopping trips.

2. Rail travel was excluded, for shopping trips by rail accounted for only 0·45 per cent of total shopping trips in the region.

3. An exponential distance function takes the form $1/\exp(cd_{ij})$, while the simple power function is, as above, $1/d_{ij}^c$.

policies: the build-up of infrastructure at the growth points, the location of new housing, and the encouragement of intra-regional migration and 'travel to work' to the designated centres. Inducements to private industry could be offered without imposing conditions about location since the social overhead capital, labour supply conditions and the avail-ability of services would attract it to the growth point.

A brief explanation needs to be given of the growth point concept to show how it reflects agglomeration as a locational determinant and the urban hierarchy system, as well as other factors such as growth pole theory and the relationship be-tween nodal centres and their zone of influence.

The basic idea of growth points is that economic activity within a region tends to agglomerate around a small number of focal points. Polarization flows will gravitate within a region towards these focal points, though the density of the flows will be reduced by distance. Around a focal point (con-trol centre, dominant node) we may delimit a boundary where the flow densities fall to a minimum critical level; the centre can be described as the growth point, while the area within the boundary is its zone of influence (or growth area). On this interpretation, the spatial distribution of population can be regarded as being organized into a hierarchical system of nodes and functional linkages. The stronger the nodal characteristics of regions the higher their growth rates and their levels of economic and social development are likely to be. Regional plans will consequently tend to be more success-ful if they effectively reinforce the natural nodal characteris-tics already in evidence in a region.[1]

A natural growth point combines the characteristics of a high-order central place and a potential location site because of agglomeration economies created there. Central place analysis and the agglomerative aspects of location have

1. An exception is where the main centres are so large and congested that a further build-up will result in severe diseconomies. In such a case the role of the planner is to select suitable locations for the stimulus of new growth points. But this is unlikely to contradict the emergent nodal structure of the region since a well-planned growth point is al-most always a potential natural growth point.

already been extensively discussed, and there is no need to dwell on them again. Large population centres have high market potential and are socially and culturally more attractive to managers, so that a growth point will normally be either a substantial population centre or capable of rapid population expansion. Most of the external economies that make some areas preferable to others are, in effect, scale economies: specialized services catering for firms in a given industry; labour market, banking and other business facilities; high rank central goods and services; and urbanization economies. The only external economies not clearly related to scale are interindustry technological economies, and this leads us on to another feature of growth points.

The modern development of growth point theory stems mainly from the work of French regional economists, particularly François Perroux.[1] Perroux has developed the concept of a *growth pole* (*pôle de croissance* or *pôle de développement*). Boudeville (1966, p. 11), paraphrasing Perroux, has defined a regional growth pole as 'a set of expanding industries located in an urban area and inducing further development of economic activity throughout its zone of influence'.

The main factor in regional expansion is interaction between key industries ('propulsive' industries) which form the nucleus of the development pole. These industries have certain characteristics: a high degree of concentration, high income elasticity of demand for their products which are usually sold to national markets, marked local multiplier and polarization effects (e.g. they probably draw most of their inputs from within the region), an advanced level of technology and managerial expertise which by the force of example are diffused to other sectors in the region.[2]

However, the growth pole implies more than the localization of key industries. It should also induce considerable

1. See Perroux (1955 and 1964). For valuable analyses in English see Hansen (1967) and Lasuen (1969).
2. The stress on technical interrelationships and agglomeration economies suggests a kinship with Isard's industrial complex analysis (Isard, Schooler and Vietorisz, 1959).

expansion in the surrounding area, and for this the strategic polarization effects are more critical than interindustry linkages. In promoting polarization, a highly developed infrastructure, provision of central services, the demand for productive factors from the zone of influence, and the spread of 'growthmindedness' and dynamism over this zone are all important.

In the selection of new growth points, other determinants have to be reckoned with. Access to abundant supplies of scarce resources, the economies attached to a transport node, nearness to an important non-transportable locational advantage (e.g. an airport) are a few of the more obvious factors influencing site selection for infrastructure investment.

The increasing returns to scale associated with growth point development are not limitless. If growth points have a critical minimum size necessary to promote expansion over the growth area as a whole, they also reach a limit beyond which net diseconomies are realized. These include urban congestion costs and the overloading of transport facilities, rising *per capita* costs of providing urban government services, and rising factor prices (particularly wages and site rents).

Efficient planning, therefore, may require the expansion of growth points to be controlled so as to maximize expansion in the surrounding zone of influence subject to efficiency constraints. The need for control is all the greater since congestion costs often fall upon society long before private business is affected. If diseconomies are incurred at a given growth point before policy objectives have been achieved, the appropriate action is to select a new growth point at considerable distance from the original one.

Growth point analysis involves the hypothesis that income will be maximized in the growth area as a whole by concentrating development at growth points rather than spreading it thinly over a whole region. The interaction between each growth point and its zone of influence is therefore an important element of the theory. This interaction has several aspects. Firstly, it implies structural imbalance over the region as a whole. If a growth point is associated with the development of a new industrial complex, it will be located around the growth point itself. Admittedly, supplying industries in the zone of influence will be stimulated, but even so there will be marked disparities in prosperity between the growth point and its surrounding area. Moreover, beyond the boundary of the zone of influence income levels may stagnate and areas decline. The justification for growth points is that these areas are bound to stagnate in any event, and that concentrating expansion results in higher average *per capita* incomes in the region as a whole.

Secondly, the propulsive industries at the growth pole are probably export industries catering for extraregional markets. Growth point theory implicitly draws upon the export base concept but gives it a spatial dimension, since the key industries are located at the growth point whereas supplying industries, labour, raw materials and dependent services may be dispersed over the zone of influence. Income received in the zone is raised by factor receipts, particularly wages earned by commuting workers. One distinction between the growth point and its zone is that the former can be regarded as the central labour market and the latter as the labour catchment area.

Thirdly, the central place function of the growth point (assuming that it is a substantial centre of population) will highlight the point–zone relationship. The provision of central services will be one of the major agglomeration economies at the growth point. But, conceptually, growth points and central places are not identical. Central places are numerous and arranged in a hierarchy, whereas there will be very few growth points – in some cases only one within a region. Polarization flows will be more intense and more varied in character around a growth point than around a central place where the flows consist mainly of commuting for shopping, leisure and other services. The most striking contrast of all is that whereas the growth of a central place is sustained by its complementary region, the growth of the zone of influence is sustained by the growth point.

Finally, a main objective in importing an advanced technological industrial complex to the growth point is to transform social attitudes over the zone of influence (e.g. higher wages making local workers more productivity-minded, outside managers helping to dispel the pessimistic expectations of indigenous businessmen and educating them to a higher level of technology). (See Hansen (1967) and James (1964).) In other words, the growth point, especially in a backward or stagnating region, is a point of entry through which dynamism and a growth mentality can be injected into the region.

Part Three The Planning Region

The third method of classifying regions (in addition to homogeneous or nodal regions) is division into planning regions. This is an essential categorization when questions of regional policy and planning arise. A planning (or programming) region is an area over which economic decisions apply, and this fact gives a unity to the area.

Since implementation of a regional policy requires the power to act, and this power rests more with governments than private agencies, then regions need to be defined as administrative areas and as political jurisdictions of various sizes and levels.[1] Economic regionalization in planned (i.e. socialist) economies, for example, means the division of a country into several parts which fulfil national objectives and also provide the foundations for regional economic administration.

Although planning regions must be taken as given, they may be badly delimited if their boundaries do not conform to the boundaries of natural economic regions. If, as is widely believed, the nodal region is the optimal planning unit, then planning decisions will be distorted if administrative regions are drawn up without regard to the functional linkages between centres, that is, if the region includes nodes which have greater interdependence with nodes outside the region. On the other hand, since planning requires statistical data, and these are normally collected on a regional basis, we have no choice other than to work with existing planning regions.

In regard to this last point, there are substantial gains to be had if data are collected on the basis of very small units (or building blocks) so that statistical information can be made to relate to any size of area. The reason for this is that the optimal planning unit will vary according to the character of the problem under investigation. Some questions, such as the selection of one centre

1. Of course, a flexible programming system will contain overlapping planning areas of different size.

for concentrating new housing in a fairly wide stagnating area containing several declining villages, can be dealt with at the sub-regional level; others, such as the design and construction of main transport arteries or the decision to develop a major irrigation or hydroelectric project, have to be tackled on a multiregional basis. Similarly, the optimal unit depends on the planning time horizon. Short-term (mainly quasi-managerial) decisions can be made within quite small areas, medium-term investment decisions (say, four to ten years) can be taken within existing regions, while the long-term development problems which call for the co-ordination of infrastructure and other basic investment require very large planning areas (possibly covering several regions). Finally, in certain circumstances spatial decentralization of the planning authority *may* offer other advantages: increased participation potential, cheaper costs of collecting, processing and transmitting information, savings in executives' time-costs, wiser and better decisions.[1]

1. For a conceptual discussion of these factors see Isard (1965).

5 Problems in Regional Planning

Predictive *v.* Planning Models

Although regional planners sometimes use predictive models aimed at forecasting the most likely course of events in the absence of intervention, they will normally wish to influence the future. In order to do this they will need to make use of a planning model. Such a model allows for specific goals and policy objectives (determined in part by the political process), and the planners via a manipulation of the instrumental variables under their control try to achieve these goals. The goals may refer either to a set of predetermined target levels (*fixed targets*) or to the maximization of some given index of welfare (*flexible target*) such as real income per head. The pursuit of the stated goals will be subject to constraints (sometimes called *boundary conditions*). These constraints, usually expressed as inequalities, may refer to fixed budgetary limits, productive capacity constraints, the available supply of labour, etc.

The essential differences between a predictive and a planning model are summarized in Figure 3. The predictive model may develop out of *a priori* theorizing alone or, more likely, from a set of behavioural assumptions, some of which at least will derive from empirical observation. Once the assumptions have been decided, the model is developed through a process of logical deduction. The model, in turn, yields predictive hypotheses which are tested empirically againt the course of events. If the results of the test are satisfactory, we may conclude that the model is consistent with experience; if there is inconsistency, on the other hand, then we must either amend the model by altering the assumptions of our theories and possibly by allowing for new observations revealed by the tests, or reject the model completely and start afresh. Since the model will almost certainly be used for forecasting future changes, the tests will have to be carried out on past as well as current data.

Predictive model   Planning model

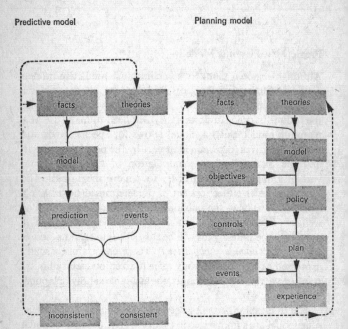

Figure 3

The planning model is used not simply for prediction, but to attempt to change events in specified directions. The model is combined with objectives formulated via the political process to derive a policy. This stage of the planning process presents problems, and the structure of the model is not necessarily independent of the objectives it is designed to serve. Consultation between politicians and the model builder is usually necessary because there is seldom one clear-cut objective and multiple objectives often conflict with each other. Moreover, meaningful objectives cannot be determined without some attention to their practicability and cost. Their selection requires adequate information and a broad assessment of social costs and benefits.

Once the policy has been decided upon, it needs to be translated into a plan. This is where the administrator comes in, because the plan is the result of combining the policy with controls (i.e. the set of administrative and operating procedures). The implementation of the plan may require some decentralization of decisions if decision costs are to be minimized, since it is expensive to transfer some kinds of information from one decision centre to another. When the plan is put into operation, it comes up against events and the result is experience. If the consequences fulfil the objectives of policy then the plan is successful. If not, then every component in each stage leading up to the plan may require modification.

Thus, the diagram shows feedbacks from experience to theories, facts, objectives and controls which carry what we learn from experience to the model, policy and plan.

Structure of the Planning Model

Let us examine the internal structure of the model stage in a little more detail. The economy is an exceedingly complex interdependent system and the planning model is a highly simplified quantitative description of it. It will contain several variables, some of which are concerned with the structural relationships which link together the separate parts of the economy (these may be called the endogenous variables), while others are predetermined (the exogenous variables), influencing the endogenous variables but not affected by them. In addition, there are the *endogenous-lagged* variables which have been predetermined in earlier time periods, but which are given at the moment that the model is being applied.

The first operation in planning is to insert into the model the goal or target variables; these may take the form of certain desired target levels or may be couched in optimization terms (i.e. a programming model where we maximize or minimize some objective function subject to constraints). The goal variables can be regarded as a special kind of exogenous variable. The next step is to find a set of values for the instrumental (or tool) variables, also exogenous, which results in desired values of the target variables. The point about the instrumental variables is that they are controllable; planning would be relatively simple if all variables could be controlled. Unfortunately, a great many variables are uncontrollable, especially *at the regional level*. These are extraneous to the region (e.g. the level of world demand for steel, or the size of the government defence budget). The regional policy-maker must assign values to these extraneous variables, and this is a major source of error. In addition, there are stochastic variables. These by definition cannot be predicted, and the usefulness of the planning model depends on their effects being very small.

A planning model of this kind can be expressed as

$$g = E(t, x, r),$$

where g = the set of outcomes,

E = endogenous variables, (i.e. the structural relationships which determine the correspondence between the independent variables and the set of outcomes),

t = instrumental variables,

x = extraneous (independent uncontrollable) variables,

and r = stochastic influences.

While g, t, x and r are vectors, E is the matrix which shows how the development of the region, as expressed in g, is linked to the instrumental and extraneous variables. The values for the endogenous coefficients in E (e.g. input–output coefficients, inter-regional trade propensities, the consumption function, the capital–output ratio) are obtained from empirical research. The instrumental variables include such things as the level of government investment in regional infrastructure, the methods of taxation, government subsidies and other items that might be manipulated by regional policy-makers to alter the outcomes. Given the structural coefficients in E and having assigned values to x, the aim of the planner is to adjust t in a manner which throws up results, expressed in g, which are consistent with policy goals.

Fixed or Flexible Targets

The choice between the efficiency of optimizing (flexible targets) and the simplicity of fixed targets is not easy to make. With the former we aim to maximize some index of welfare or growth (such as the rate of growth in regional income per head) or minimize the real costs of achieving an objective subject to specified constraints. This approach is efficient because we are able to compare the advantages gained with the costs of the policy, and adopt the course of action which results in the maximum present value of benefits less costs; this depends on both the target *and* the instrumental variables.

The disadvantage of this type of model is that it can normally cope only with narrow, measurable goals and cannot handle many multiple goals since its basic technique is to optimize a primary goal, relegating other goals to constraints.[1] Fixed targets are less efficient and, as we shall see, may give rise to the problem of matching instruments with targets. On the other hand, they are simpler and more practicable and a large number of goals can be aimed for, provided that they are not contradictory.

Conditions for a Solution

Another problem is the conditions under which a planning model yields a solution. Tinbergen (1952 and 1954) showed that in well-constructed economic models the number of structural relations (equations) will be equal to the total number of unknowns. He also demonstrated that with flexible targets in the general case where the number of instruments exceeds the number of targets, there will be a maximizing solution which can be found from the almost limitless possibilities. With fixed targets, however, for an effective solution the number of targets must equal the number of instruments. Too many instruments create problems, while if targets exceed

1. In a brilliant article, however, Leven (1964) showed that a programming model can maximize multiple goals if they are few in number and closely related.

instruments the model yields no solution. Moreover, the boundary conditions (or constraints) may interfere with the operation of the planning model. A policy is inconsistent when the required values of the instrumental variables needed to achieve the stated goals are infeasible due to boundary conditions. In such a case either some of the constraints must be relaxed or the targets must be revised downwards.

Regional Compared with National Planning

Discussions sometimes imply that regional planning is simply a miniature version of national economic planning. Such an analogy must not be pushed too far. The introduction of a space dimension results in a substantial increase in the variables and equations in economic models. For operationality, the number of sectors and regions has usually to be restricted severely, and one region in the model has to be reserved for the 'rest-of-the-world' sector. Moreover, once location is a variable, planning must be concerned not only with the allocation of resources among sectors and regions but also *within* regions; thus, regional planning almost always includes a physical planning component.

Regions are clearly more open economies than nations, and this high degree of openness has certain repercussions on regional planning: firstly, policy instruments are less effective because of spillovers outside regional boundaries; secondly, data on inter-regional economic relations (especially trade coefficients) are sketchy and very imperfect. This is one aspect of a more general problem of data limitations, since regional statistics are very sparse apart from population and employment estimates. The effectiveness of planning depends on enough information being available where and as it is required. As for instruments, regional planning requires a different set from those employed at the national level, and since experience with them is more limited, their effects are less predictable. Finally, as suggested above, there are more exogenous variables in a regional model; although some of these can be manipulated by the central government others cannot.

Obviously, the larger the number of exogenous variables outside the control of planners the more difficult the task of manipulating the instrumental variables to achieve the targets required.[1]

All these differences may reduce the usefulness of econometric type planning models for regional policy, at least in the near future.[2] This conclusion is magnified when the models employed rely on relationships that are assumed to be linear.[3]

Goal Conflicts

The regional planning problem is complicated by the fact that in most cases a region will not be allowed to pursue its own objectives regardless of their effect on national efficiency or on the aims of other regions. The objectives of an individual region may conflict with those of its neighbours and with those of the national economy. Broadly speaking, a regional policy normally has both a growth and an equity component – that is, it is concerned with stimulating growth and efficiency in the national economy *and* with narrowing marked inter-regional disparities in welfare indices. But these may contradict each other since maximizing real *per capita* national income may do nothing towards equalizing regional income differentials. Indeed, the sum of maximized regional incomes is equal to maximized national income only in a world of perfect competition.

One solution, then, might be to attempt to recreate the conditions of perfect competition. Lefeber (1958), for example, suggests the application of certain basic marginal cost pricing rules as a guide for the regional planner. The drawbacks of this approach are: a stable dynamic general equilibrium may

1. Some variables (e.g. the price or wage level, import duties and government subsidies) may be instrumental variables for the central government but an exogenous variable for the regional planner.
2. This is the argument put forward by Klaassen (1965, p. 24).
3. For a recent discussion of the pitfalls arising from a careless use of linear models see Colenutt (1968).

be impossible; the price mechanism may not be an efficient spatial allocator, mainly due to indivisibilities; it ignores the problems arising from the theory of second best.

Goal conflicts are the rule not the exception. The regional growth process is probably unbalanced because of agglomeration economies, indivisibilities in investment, differences in resource endowment, and the uneven spatial distribution of population and market demand. Thus pursuit of growth and efficiency is likely to cause trouble when equity objectives are important. Usually some sort of compromise will have to be sought. It has recently been shown how, theoretically, trade-offs may be derived between efficiency and inter-regional equity (Mera, 1967).

In practice, some kind of balance will have to be struck, though efficiency goals will naturally tend to be uppermost in the minds of the national planner, and regional and equity goals given priority by the regional planner. For instance, in a national planning model the primary objective may be to maximize some index of national economic welfare subject to certain regional constraints (such as ensuring that the slowest growing regions develop at least as fast as the national economy). The regional planner, on the other hand, will be concerned primarily with planning for the individual region. It is not sufficient for the national planner to choose investment projects which yield an excess of social benefits over social costs. In project evaluation he should always consider the opportunity costs as measured by the returns to factors in alternative uses. Moreover, since a given end can often be achieved by any one of several means, he should select from the available instrumental variables that which interferes least with the most efficient allocation of resources.

Contradictions between the goals of different regions are also common. Measures taken by policy-makers in one region (e.g. devices to restrict out-migration) may prevent the achievement of objectives in other regions. Regions may compete with each other in lobbying the central government for preferential treatment in the location of government investments, and success may depend more on political pressure than on efficiency. The proper inference from problems of this kind is that regional policy-makers should not be given too much independence, and that the central government must be the arbiter among regions. However, if regional preferences differ this may give rise to a 'ranking of goals' problem. Fortunately, this is not insoluble; the state may intervene and by following certain procedures make the regions agree (Boudeville, 1966, pp. 123–35).

6 The Direction of Regional Policy

Intervention in regional economic affairs by the central government has in most countries involved something rather less than inter-regional planning on a systematic basis. The choice has very often been between reliance on market forces to allocate resources and on subsidies for the movement of labour and/or of capital.

To discuss the problems of lagging regions in terms of a 'labour out, jobs in' choice in the selection of instruments, is to oversimplify the issues facing the regional policy-maker. In the first place, the broad direction of regional policy depends on goals. For instance, if national efficiency is the chief goal it may be better to promote inter-regional migration of labour rather than to persuade industry to relocate; but if satisfying locational preferences ranks high in goal priorities more emphasis may be placed on inducing capital to move. Secondly, the 'labour out, jobs in' approach almost implies that the regional problem is one of local labour market disequilibria and that eliminating regional unemployment differentials is the main objective of regional policy.

But regional measures may be concerned with other goals both regional and national, and depressed regions may face quite different problems and require different treatment according to whether they are stagnant industrial or underdeveloped rural regions. Thus, there is no general solution applicable in all circumstances. However, since the choice between intervention and non-intervention and between subsidies to capital and to labour has been extensively, if not always clearly, discussed by economists and policy-makers, we must give the question some attention here.

The Market as an Allocator

There is a school of thought which believes that the operation of market forces offers the least cost and a reasonably acceptable solution to regional economic problems. The arguments used to support this viewpoint include: the evidence of convergence in *per capita* incomes in advanced economies (particularly the United States) over historical periods in which there was no direct regional intervention; the opinion that man-made regulators are too inflexible to replace the often minute spatial differentials in costs, prices and incomes resulting from the general interdependence of the space economy; the suggestion that if decision-making is spread among a large number of individual firms, rather than being centralized, then forecasting errors will tend to cancel out. The liberal economist is not necessarily opposed to all intervention. He may be in favour of increasing competition in the space economy via 'lubrication' (i.e. using the price mechanism to reallocate resources).[1]

However, we can criticize the market as a regional allocator. The general equilibrium theory upon which it is based tends to be static, whereas the regional process is dynamic. The argument assumes perfect competition and marginalism, neither of which is very relevant to the space economy; oligopoly and monopoly are more typical spatial market forms, while locational changes usually involve either a long distance jump or no move at all rather than a marginal shift. Location decisions may also be based on irrationality and made in ignorance of relevant knowledge.

Even if regional economic trends exhibit equilibrating tendencies, the path of adjustment may be very painful. The market mechanism may be rejected because of divergences between social and private costs and returns, such as social congestion costs in centres of agglomeration. In some cases,

1. For example, we might include under this heading the regional payroll tax-rebate schemes put forward by Colin Clark. See Clark and Peters (1964) and Clark (1966). For a more recent contribution see Hutton and Hartley (1968).

it wastes resources; for instance, it fails to reap the potential gains from investment in migration or to employ immobile out-of-work workers in their home region. Finally, *laissez-faire* may be politically unacceptable, regardless of its efficiency, if it perpetuates rather than eliminates regional disparities in incomes and employment opportunities.

Subsidies to Migrants

The effects of migration on origin and destination regions can vary widely according to the characteristics of the regions concerned and the composition of the migration stream (Okun and Richardson, 1961, ch. 9). The justification for measures to induce migration will also depend on policy objectives, but there is little doubt that in some circumstances aid to migrants is appropriate. Measures may take two main forms. Firstly, subsidies for education and retraining will indirectly induce mobility. Such subsidies are often consistent with efficiency since individuals may underinvest in themselves because of ignorance, capital market imperfections and divergences between social and private returns. Secondly, direct financial assistance may be given to migrants. This may be required even where inter-regional income differentials are large because migration costs may be heavy. It is possible to calculate a rate of return on migration which may be compared with returns from other investments (Sjaastad, 1962; Richardson, 1969, ch. 12).

The argument in favour of a regional policy geared to inducing the inter-regional movement of labour is that it will result in a better balance between regional supplies of labour and employment opportunities. Aggregate output will increase because the level of employment will rise and workers will in many cases move from low to high productivity industries. Moreover, in most instances (such as the conditions prescribed by a neo-classical model) inter-regional income differentials will be reduced. Its proponents argue that such a policy is not only consistent with national efficiency but also eliminates the stagnation characteristics of depressed regions – high unemployment and low income.

The arguments of those who oppose this type of policy are in the main unconvincing. They are often expounded as if they were valid in all cases, rather than being possible outcomes in some, often unlikely, conditions. The alleged adverse effects of migration refer to regions of destination and of origin. In regard to the former, one familiar argument is that the marginal social costs of an in-migrant exceed his contribution to local taxes; an often quoted example is rising marginal costs in the supply of public services when the migrant pays only the average costs. This line of analysis is open to objections. Even if the marginal social costs of migration exceed marginal private costs, this may be outweighed by marginal social benefits. Since migrants and locals pay the same price for public services, then a failure by migrants to pay their marginal costs simply means that the pricing method is faulty and not that migration is inefficient. Moreover, rising marginal costs of services imply that certain services have less than perfectly elastic supply functions, and suppliers of these services will in fact gain by any rise in prices associated with migration. Of course, there may still be technological external diseconomies created by in-migration, such as air pollution and overcrowding.

Another argument is that migration into prosperous regions aggravates inflationary tendencies rather than, as common sense might suggest, relieves them. This belief rests on the assumption that in-migration adds more to investment demand than to savings and more to the demand for labour than to supply. But the effects on demand and on supply are not felt simultaneously. The immediate effect is to increase labour supply. It may be that eventually this may be more than outweighed by the effects of migrants on investment in housing and social services provision and on the derived demand for labour; but before this is felt the supply position will have had time to readjust. In the short run, migrants will merely use existing services so that these are used more intensively.

Moreover, the effect depends on the type of inflation. In-migration is more likely to aggravate inflation if it is of the demand-pull variety, but will tend to reduce it if the source of inflation is rising labour costs.

The adverse effects of out-migration on regions of origin are often described melodramatically: underutilization of social capital and a higher *per capita* burden, excess capacity in private industry, downward multiplier effects on local service industries, decline in the quality of the labour force, loss of investments in educated migrants, and the withdrawal of capital. These consequences are in fact usually negligible or non-existent. Social capital may be poor, requiring replacement, or overutilized; private capital may be obsolete and should be scrapped so that resources required for its replacement can be put to more productive use elsewhere; if out-migrants consist of the unemployed or low-income families the *per capita* fiscal burden will fall as social security payments are reduced; out-migrants may send remittances from their new areas.

Subsidies for the migration of women may be unjustified and ineffective. Since married women desire work only for a limited fraction of their life, the discounted income gain may be too low to justify moving. A region may adequately employ its male labour force but have a large surplus of tied female labour. In this case, activity rates can only be raised by providing jobs in the region.[1] This is an economic argument against the migration solution which may be valid in some circumstances.

Another justification for moving jobs rather than workers is that the costs of urban development (e.g. providing basic infrastructure, housing and services) for an expanding population may be higher in areas potentially attractive to migrants than in areas of origin.[2] The strongest argument, however, may be social. If the satisfaction of locational preferences

1. Regional differences in female activity rates are, in fact, very large in the U.K.
2. This type of problem could be analysed in threshold cost terms. See Kozlowski and Hughes (1967 and 1968) and Malisz (1969).

ranks high in society's scale of values, an electorally conscious government would be foolish to frustrate these preferences by inducing migration for possibly marginal efficiency gains.

Policies to Change the Location of Industry

Influencing the location of capital and new industry has these days a much wider appeal than stimulating inter-regional migration, so much so that very few observers recognize that acting on both fronts may be complementary rather than contradictory. The arguments used to justify intervention in the location of industry are of varying merit. Let us briefly consider a few of them. If, as is often suggested, a large proportion of modern industry is 'footloose' and spatial differences in costs are small, then perhaps intervention in location may be excused. But managerial efficiency and location may be interdependent, and efficiency may be harmed if managers are induced to move from locations which yield them psychic income. The above-mentioned social argument that inducing capital to move may satisfy individual locational preferences has an economic counterpart in the case where substantial inducements to migrate fail to persuade people to move. If these people are unemployed in their home region, social benefits are derived from finding work for them. National output will be raised through their employment, and the costs involved may be consistent with efficiency provided that capital is not diverted from much more productive uses elsewhere. Another argument is that inducing the relocation of industry into lagging regions will make for an improved 'regional balance'. The concept of regional balance is too subjective and nebulous in most discussions to give it much consideration; but one aspect worthy of attention is that there may be marked complementarities in inter-regional development, so that a regional system composed of regions of similar size and income levels may grow faster than where one or two regions dwarf the rest.

Most of the other arguments for intervention on the capital front are not convincing, though they may hold in particular circumstances. For instance, it is sometimes argued that policy-makers should attempt to solve the problems of stagnant regions by rectifying their unfavourable industrial composition. A diagnosis of this kind suffers from excessive simplification. Some depressed regions may be rural. The economic performance of an industrial region may not be determined by its industrial composition as such, and *differential* effects may be much more important than *proportional* effects (Perloff, Dunn, Lampard and Muth, 1960). Moreover, even if improving its activity mix is relevant to remedying a region's problems this is a long-run solution, and in the short run, when raising the level of employment may be the chief goal, measures will have to be confined to subsidies to existing industries or to migrants.

Another alleged justification for intervention is that inducing locational transfers to the less prosperous regions would reduce external diseconomies of congestion in the rapidly growing, highly urbanized regions. Although not necessarily wrong, this argument is easily exaggerated. For instance, it only applies to technological external diseconomies. Moreover, since congested cities are found in almost all regions the relief of congestion is much more of an *intra*regional than an inter-regional problem.

It is sometimes suggested that subsidies should be given to enable firms in problem regions to benefit from increasing returns to scale and external agglomeration economies. This suggestion is more relevant to rural underdeveloped regions, though it may justify temporary subsidies towards creating a new industrial complex, even in an old-established industrial region, provided that opportunity-cost criteria are satisfied.

This leads on to a consideration of the criteria upon which a location-of-industry policy should be judged. Obviously, the selection of criteria cannot be divorced from policy objectives. Assuming that growth in *per capita* income or related measures is more important than a reduction in unemployment, then subsidies to firms at specific locations should be judged in terms of future income growth or the generation of external economies rather than in terms of the number of jobs created and their cost. For example, inducing the transfer of a plant *and* all its workers may be justified even though few jobs are created provided that the transfer leads to an inflow of other firms.

The pursuit of efficiency should also play some role in the determination of criteria. This is most easily accommodated by including the opportunity cost of an investment in any subsidy evaluation. It also suggests the desirability, where practicable, of selective inducements rather than blanket subsidies to all firms in all industries. For instance, there may be a case for higher subsidies to certain types of industry such as those giving rise to local factor receipts and producing goods for export or goods for which demand is highly income elastic.

Finally, we must mention briefly some of the methods available for attracting capital into problem regions. Negative controls in the form of restrictions on plant expansions and new capital developments in prosperous regions may be employed, but they should not be used indiscriminately. Although their budget cost is negligible, they may give rise to heavy real costs as measured by sacrifices in efficiency. Even more extreme is to give directives to industrialists to go to certain areas, but these are widely regarded as unacceptable in a liberal democracy. More favoured solutions are to counteract agglomeration trends in private capital with an offsetting movement of public funds to depressed regions and/or to subsidize private industry there. The range of measures available is very broad: the provision of information; increasing the supply of basic services and infrastructure at locations selected for development; investment in education and retraining; price-fixing powers in public utilities which can affect regional location; regional discrimination in government contracts and other items of public capital expenditure; financial inducements to firms which include investment allowances, grants, loans or tax rebates; the selection of growth points.

The choice of instruments will depend partly on policy objectives and partly on their effectiveness in given institutional environments. It is consequently almost impossible to generalize. Borts (1966) argued that wage subsidies are more efficient than capital or price subsidies, but his analysis depends on the critical assumption that capital is the variable and labour the fixed factor. Moreover, wage subsidies are inappropriate for rural regions, for which the solution is to induce labour out of agriculture into the migration stream or into local high-productivity industries. On the other hand, investment subsidies result in a greater than efficient utilization of capital.[1]

Of the different forms of subsidy to capital, tax concessions, though they have the advantage of rewarding the efficient, are probably less successful than initial investment grants which help relocating firms when they need help most. Moreover, automatic subsidies are more highly regarded by time-conscious firms than those which have to be negotiated. Capital subsidies can be granted without any specific locational guidance provided that they are combined with a growth point policy. The build-up of infrastructure, and the physical planning of housing and transport near to potential industrial sites, will in themselves attract industry to the growth points, so that financial inducements can be made location free.

Location-of-Industry Policy in Britain

Surveys of location-of-industry policy in Britain abound, and there is no need to cover this well-trodden ground here.[2] Aid

1. There is some evidence that the ratio of investment per man in development areas to investment per man elsewhere is higher in capital-intensive industries, so that the bias in favour of subsidies to capital (reduced but not eliminated by the introduction of the Regional Employment Premium) seems to attract capital- rather than labour-intensive industries to the lagging regions. See *Annual Report by the Board of Trade under the Industrial Development Act, 1966* (1968).

2. The most comprehensive study is by McCrone (1969). Other sources include Hemming (1963), Loasby (1965 and 1967), Needleman and Scott (1964), Thirlwall (1966), Miernyk (1966), Bird and Thirlwall (1967), Wilson (1967). For a clear descriptive but uncritical summary of policy changes see Dowie (1968).

to depressed areas was started in 1934 in conditions of general unemployment, but dispersal-of-industry policies were really consequent upon the findings of the Barlow Commission in 1940.[1] Policy up to the late 1950s was administered under the Distribution of Industry Act of 1945 (amended in 1958) and the Town and Country Planning Act of 1947.

The areas that could benefit from aid were reduced under the Local Employment Act of 1960, but the geographical and financial scope of assistance was broadened by legislation after 1963.[2] Over this period there have been considerable changes in the areas eligible for assistance and in the type and scale of subsidy offered. The most revolutionary change in area status took place in 1966 when the old localized development districts were replaced by geographically large development areas.[3] Although this was a reversion to a size of development area in existence between 1945 and 1960, it also – and this was its most important feature – marked a shift in emphasis from local to regional planning. Moreover, development areas could for the first time be created for reasons other than high unemployment such as unfavourable demographic changes (e.g. high rates of net out-migration).

The present set of measures in operation to influence the location of industry include the following: 40 per cent cash grants for plant and machinery compared with 20 per cent elsewhere (*or* an initial investment allowance of 30 per cent),

1. *Report of the Royal Commission on the Distribution of the Industrial Population* (Cmnd 6153, 1940).

2. The Local Employment Act and the Finance Act of 1963, the Control of Office and Industrial Development Act of 1965, and the Industrial Development Act and the Finance Act of 1966.

3. In the recent report of the Hunt Committee, *The Intermediate Areas*, H.M.S.O., April 1969, it was recommended that financial aid in the way of 25 per cent industrial building grants should be extended to all 'grey' areas, particularly the North Western and Yorkshire and Humberside regions. The government, however, has agreed to assist only seven limited areas out of savings made by withdrawing the Selective Employment Premium from the development areas. In a note of dissent to the Hunt Report, A. J. Brown argued the case for a broader classification of areas – including development areas, grey areas, neutral areas and congested areas (the latter to pay a congestion tax) – on the lines of the system operating in France.

and these grants are available for all new projects in manufacturing and extractive industries regardless of their
employment-creating effect; building grants of 25 per cent
(35 per cent in special circumstances) which could be given to
service industries as well as manufacturing (provided more
than fifty jobs were created); provision of advance factories
for sale or lease at attractive rates; discretionary loans and
grants including from 1966 the possibility that the Board of
Trade could subscribe to shares or stock, or make loans with
an option to convert into equities; resettlement and removal
grants for workers (these are little used); grants to local
authorities to rehabilitate derelict land and improve basic
public services; controls on factory development (and from
November 1964 of office building) in prosperous regions
under Industrial Development Certificates; last but not least,
from September 1967 a wage subsidy (Regional Employment
Premium) of 30s. was given for each adult male manufacturing employee in the development areas for at least seven
years, with lower rates for women, juveniles and part-timers.[1]

We have already mentioned some of the general points that
can be made about measures of this kind: the hidden costs of
negative controls; the preference for firms for automatic,
initial subsidies and the contrary argument that financial
assistance should stimulate initiative whereas cash grants and
wage subsidies are unconditional; the capital bias despite
R.E.P. of existing subsidies.

Let us here confine our remarks to an over-all assessment
of the degree of success of these policies. There is no doubt that
policy has held the gap in regional unemployment and *per
capita* income differentials in check, but the convergence
tendencies have been imperceptible rather than striking. The
development areas accounting for about 20 per cent of the
insured population have absorbed over half of the total re-
locations in recent years, and have taken over half the additional employment resulting from i.d.c. approval.[2] Up to
1965, however, when restrictions were tightened, many small

1. An additional subsidy of 7s. 6d. (the Selective Employment Premium) was withdrawn in April 1970.
2. For further details see Howard (1968).

but important developments and many plant expansions escaped the net. Other loop-holes were closed in 1966, but even so i.d.c. policy has had only a fair degree of success and many concerns forced to relocate, particularly office developments, have moved to new sites outside the development areas.

The appraisal of i.d.c. policy is a difficult task, because we know very little about its costs in terms of losses in efficiency to be set against the benefits. The benefits can easily be exaggerated; the official estimate of manpower gain from reducing regional unemployment and increasing activity rates is equivalent to 2 per cent of the national labour force.[1]

Moreover, the financial costs of assistance have increased in recent years. Between 1945 and 1960 the Board of Trade spent £77·7 million on factory building and industrial estates while the Treasury spent £12 million in loans and grants. In the seven years ending March 1967, loans and grants totalled £89·5 million, building and plant grants £76·3 million and government factory building £64·8 million. The wage subsidies in operation since September 1967 amount to about £125 million annually, and the total annual cost of all government financial assistance to the development areas including investment allowances is about £260 million.

Although policy measures have had some success in diverting growth from the South-East and Midlands, the flow of new jobs has not kept pace with the flow of migrants in the opposite direction. The creation of new jobs in the development areas is probably less than the rundown in primary and extractive industries and in declining manufacturing sectors. Given that the size of the labour force is also increasing, relative stability could not be maintained without the outflow of migrants.

Some observers have criticized the present structure of aid on the grounds that the explicit link between the scale of assistance and the creation of new jobs has been broken. But if

1. As J. R. Cable points out (Prest, 1968, p. 167) the increase in output could be less, depending on the capital–labour ratio and on the relative productivity of female and male labour, since a high proportion of the increase in employment would consist of women.

long-run capacity for growth is an important policy objective, demonstration effects and the build-up of agglomeration and other external economies are more important than short-run boosts to the level of employment. There is a case, on the other hand, for a more direct 'matching' of industries with areas. There has been very little research into the locational advantages and disadvantages of regions for particular industries, yet this may determine whether transplants are successful or not. However, a plea for selectivity in regard to steering specific industries to specific regions should not be read as implying that financial assistance should always be made conditional and offered at discretionary levels.

The level and types of assistance available at present makes, as we have seen, for a rather complicated structure of incentives. Simpler, more straightforward forms of aid, more heavily publicized, may be important to the success of a location-of-industry policy especially if location decisions are based on 'satisficing' or other non-profit-maximizing behaviour.

Regional Planning Bodies and Their Reports

A comparatively recent development (April 1965) in British regional policy is the establishment of regional planning bodies, the Regional Economic Planning Councils, which are made up of private persons acting as individuals but reflecting varied interests within each region, and the Planning Boards comprising civil servants. At the time, their establishment seemed to mark a turning-point in regional policy, switching emphasis from eliminating regional unemployment differentials towards showing how each region might best contribute to the performance of the national economy. It has not worked out like this. Disenchantment with national planning has left the Regional Councils and Planning Boards in a vacuum; moreover, preoccupation with national balance of payments and related problems meant very low priority for regional questions. Since the Councils have no powers (these remain with the central government and local authorities) they can only operate effectively if policy-makers offer direction and leadership.

The terms of reference for the councils were: to assist in the formulation of regional plans, having regard to the best use of the region's resources; to advise on steps necessary to implement such plans with the aid of information provided by the planning board; and to advise on the regional implications of national economic policies. In view of what has happened, this was too ambitious. The early work of the regional bodies has been concerned with describing the region's structure and amenities, forecasting population and employment changes, stating the regional priorities and suggesting how the government could assist in promoting the region's objectives. What they have not done is to draw up a set of dovetailing regional plans. Indeed, as we shall see, there has been a tendency on the part of many Councils to ignore the objectives of adjacent or competing regions and to indulge in selfish bids for the undivided attention of the government. It is, of course, true that inter-regional conflicts of objectives have to be reconciled by the government through the decisions that it takes, but the Councils have done little to point out these conflicts and suggest workable compromises.

The problems of regional imbalance, and the regional implications of national economic planning (if and when it is revived) need supraregional solutions; and the regional bodies can only participate as agents of the central government. This does not mean that there is nothing for them to do in the present environment. Firstly, they can co-ordinate and promote research into regional problems. Secondly, as Sargent (1968) has reminded us, there is a pressing need to give physical planning a regional dimension and an economic framework. Here, the Planning Councils have an important function, for they can provide the wider context for physical planning decisions. Public authorities have control over land use and the powers to carry through physical planning proposals. The central preoccupation of physical planners has been to provide housing for an increased population in a way which reduces urban congestion costs. But this is only one aspect of a much wider problem of how to achieve the optimal spatial distribution of population and economic activity. The regional planning bodies can act as a link between the local authorities whose primary interest is in the narrower questions (e.g. overspill decisions) and the central government, with its interest in national efficiency. Moreover, the planning bodies can work out the physical planning implications of public and private economic decisions in so far as they affect the region. Up to the present, these functions have not been exercised to any great extent. The sponsorship of research and acting as a forum for the raising of regional problems have been more important activities.

The first fruit of the regional planning bodies has been a series of reports on the present structure and future of each region.[1] These reports have not been planning documents but preliminary surveys and predictive studies. They have been preoccupied with several broad topics: a general outline of the structural characteristics of the region; forecasts of population

1. These include *The North-West: A Regional Study* (1965) and Appendix, *The Problems of Merseyside*; *The West Midlands: A Regional Study* (1965) and *The West Midlands: Patterns of Growth* (1967); *The Challenge of the Changing North* (1966); *A Strategy for the South-East* (1967); *A Region with a Future: A Draft Strategy for the South-West* (1967); *A Review of Yorkshire and Humberside* (1966); *The East Midlands Study* (1966); *Wales: The Way Ahead* (Cmnd 3334, 1967) and *East Anglia: A Survey* (1968). For Scotland an over-all survey *The Scottish Economy 1965 to 1970* (Cmnd 2864, 1966) has been followed by a number of regional studies including *The Lothians Regional Survey and Plan* (2 vols, 1966), *The Grangemouth Falkirk Study* (2 vols, 1968), *The Central Borders: A Plan for Expansion* (2 vols, 1968), and *North-East Scotland: A Survey of its Development Potential* (1969). Also relevant though not connected with the establishment of the regional planning bodies are *Central Scotland: A Programme for Development and Growth* (Cmnd 2188, 1963), *The North-East: A Programme for Regional Development and Growth* (Cmnd 2206, 1963), *The South-East Study 1961–81* (1964) and *Economic Development in Northern Ireland* (Cmnd 479, 1965). The regional planning bodies are in the process of working on and publishing extensions to their initial ideas. See for instance *An Outline Strategy of Development to 1981* (April 1969) by the Northern Economic Planning Council, while an interdepartmental planning team (the Burns team) is at present evaluating alternative strategies available for the development of the South-East region.

change and employment; discussion of housing problems and estimation of housing need; and the implications of regional growth for population distribution within the region.

We have already suggested that planning within each region should not be considered in isolation from what happens in adjacent regions or from national growth priorities. The regional studies have tended almost unanimously to neglect this broader context, though they have differed in the lip-service paid to it. At one extreme, we have the East Midlands study stating that its primary purpose is to ensure that the region makes its maximum contribution to national prosperity; at the other, the report of the Northern Economic Planning Council which strikes a more propagandist note stressing the promotion of the claims of the Northern Region for preferential treatment by the government. This report was typical in its complete neglect of the repercussions of growth in the region on what happens elsewhere, except in regard to road programmes and the selection of an international airport for the north of England. In some cases, for instance the West Midlands study, the wider national context of regional expansion (in this case expansion into the less densely populated western zone) was consciously underplayed and attention concentrated on the local physical pattern of development.

The case made out by individual regions to justify consistency with national objectives is usually based on the principle that maximizing growth in a region ensures that the region makes its fullest contribution to national growth.[1] This clearly ignores opportunity-cost criteria.

The regional studies contain useful statistical information about economic performance in each region, and this is no place to summarize the reports in general. It may be useful, however, to offer brief comments on two questions. Firstly, are these reports consistent with each other? Secondly, what do they have to say about the selection of growth points? These questions relate to the vexing problem of goal conflicts

1. Again, the Northern Economic Planning Council is the strongest adherent to this view, but the other Councils also appear to support it in different degrees.

discussed earlier and to the specialization of the Councils and Boards in the intraregional spatial and physical planning aspects of development.

Inconsistencies between the various studies do not appear to be very serious, despite the failure to co-ordinate and inte-grate their results with national and other regional projections. This probably reflects the generalizations that abound in the reports, and contradictions may emerge in future reports when they descend to details. In regard to population pro-jections, for example, the total individual regional forecasts amount to only about half a million more than the Registrar General's aggregate forecast for Great Britain over the period 1966–81 (a difference of about 7 per cent). Given the uncer-tainties attached to regional migration estimates this is a very satisfactory result. No doubt it is helped by the fact that most of the reports took the Registrar General's estimates as a starting point, and by the realization that regional population projections are one area where inter-regional aspects cannot be ignored. Thus, the South-West study states explicitly that its population forecasts depend on in-migration and that the rate of this depends on the success of policies pursued in other regions to reduce their net migration rates.[1]

In other respects, the myopic intraregional approach has more dubious results. For instance, each of the studies considers rehousing of its overspill and additional population in terms of new towns and other sites for housing within its own borders, and this may conflict with the optimal location of overspill developments from the national point of view.[2]

The potentially most significant addition to the dimensions of regional policy and planning in recent years has been growth point analysis. It is interesting to observe how far the regional studies take this line of approach. Although most of them have something to say about the regional distribution of population, it is revealing that the selection of centres is closely tied up

1. *A Region with a Future: A Draft Strategy for the South-West* (1967, p. 83).
2. The South-East region is an exception to this generalization.

with the need to provide houses for overspill development and not with choosing centres for industrial growth.[1] Of course, there is nothing inherently contradictory in these two aspects; indeed, in most cases, houses and jobs have to be located near together. But in these reports, new towns and housing sites are chosen primarily because they are suitable for housing development and not because they have long-term growth potential due to low-cost advantages or incipient agglomeration economies.

The 1964 South-East study goes furthest towards suggesting that criteria for selection of new centres for overspill population should relate to broader growth objectives. It suggested that selected places should have sound prospects of rapid growth and in particular should be able to attract commerce and offices from London. Other criteria should include distance from London, access to major communications networks, physical planning requirements (water availability, the avoidance of good agricultural land, etc.) and economies of scale (centres in excess of 100,000 population are probably necessary to support first-class services).

Most of the post-1965 reports have little to say on the selection of specific centres for housing *and* industrial development. In the choice of centres they tend to choose too many, usually because decisions are based simply on whether the housing and population can be accommodated, or areas which are too broad (where selection is influenced by the capacity for regional growth) such as the Carlisle–Solway area, the Lothians or Tees-side. In only a few rare cases are specific criteria introduced: for instance, in the North-West the choice of 'Ribbleton' (Leyland–Chorley) was influenced by its strategic position relative to the motorway network.

Some of the studies, particularly those for Yorkshire and

1. The Hunt Report, on the other hand, recommended a growth zone approach emphasizing industrial expansion to meet the problems of the North-West and Yorkshire and Humberside (paras. 439–56, esp. 443). In his note of dissent, however, A. J. Brown thought these areas were unsuitable for this type of policy (paras. 10–15, pp. 157–9).

Humberside, the East Midlands and the South-West, scarcely mention growth points at all. Growth point analysis has probably been developed more in Scotland, not surprisingly since the concept was pioneered there – at least as far as the U.K. is concerned. For example, the Central Borders Plan lists several reasons why the major expansion up to the 1980s should be based on St Boswells: it has the greatest long-run growth potential, suitable level sites for industrial development, good access to all existing population centres, is close to Galashiels (the main focus of population), it is near to the best national route – the A68 trunk road, it is one of the least expensive areas to develop[1] and the build-up of public utility services there is economically justified.

1. As suggested by threshold cost analysis; see Hughes and Kozlowski (1968).

7 Some Regional Planning Techniques

We have already discussed briefly a few of the more basic techniques of regional analysis: regional multipliers, economic base studies, graph analysis, gravity models, growth point analysis, decision and planning models generally.[1] It is appropriate at this final stage of the book to fill in some of the most obvious gaps on the techniques side. These include regional accounting systems, linear programming, input–output analysis, technique for area planning, comparative cost studies, industrial complex analysis, cost–benefit studies and systems analysis. Their survey must necessarily be very sketchy, and readers are urged to consult the specialist literature.[2] We attempt to do little more than give a general appraisal of their scope and limitations, and detailed description of each technique and examination of its methodology have both had to be sacrificed for considerations of space.

Regional Accounts

It is sometimes argued that the construction of sets of regional accounts is an essential prerequisite before regional planning can be undertaken.[3] If this is the case, then regional accounting methods must be regarded as a *technique* of analysis. However, the need for regional accounts can easily be exaggerated, though this is not to say that they do not have their uses. Their minimum value is to provide a foundation for regional

1. See above, pp. 19–36, 68, 97–107, 111–116.
2. For guides to this see Isard (1960), Isard and Cumberland (1961), Gibbs (1961) and Chapin (1965).
3. McCrone (1968), for example, appears to subscribe to this view.

economic analysis in the same way as national accounting lays a base for the study of macroeconomic theory. Moreover, because of their greater precision, accounting data can fulfil a valuable service by compelling theorists to define their concepts and to fit their theories into a framework consistent with the collection of statistics.

Thus, regional accounts can aid regional theorists by supplying a consistency-checking device and by promoting the construction of operational models. It is also true that regional accounting systems provide a helpful framework for the policy-maker; they give a base of information for decision making and they facilitate 'impact evaluation' studies (i.e. tracing the repercussions of changes in economic activity through the regional economy).

The trouble is that the data requirements for regional accounting systems are so heavy, and so much of the information required is inaccessible, that the heavy cost of constructing a workable set of accounts is difficult to justify. The data needed by the policy-maker for effective planning can, if supported by some of the techniques of analysis which are available, be much less than the information called for by regional accounts. For example, whereas national accounts may often assume a closed economy, regional accounts can never afford this luxury since inter-regional flows are at the heart of regional analysis. Moreover, as already noted, one of the major uses to which regional accounts would be put is to trace the impact of external forces on local production. Thus, inter-regional accounts must contain estimates of regional imports and exports, yet in most countries (apart from a few of those organized federally) most inter-regional transactions go unrecorded.

Another statistical difficulty is that there is often a large difference between regional income received and regional domestic product, partly because workplaces and residences may lie on opposite sides of a regional boundary, partly because of extraregional ownership of capital. Even more serious is the need to include a central government account in any meaningful regional accounting system, not only to assess the impact of regional policy and government investment but also because taxes have regionally differentiated effects. Finally, to the extent that regional accounts are desirable, it is not at all clear that the income accounts characteristic of national accounting systems are the most appropriate. The industrial breakdown of a region may be more useful than division into income components. Because income spillovers are hard to trace, a regional breakdown of interindustry sales and purchases may be easier to obtain than regional income flows.

Despite their drawbacks and the fact that they also require huge amounts of data, regional input–output accounts may be cheaper and more valuable than income accounts (Cao-Pinna, 1961).

Linear Programming

Linear programming is an optimizing technique. It relates to problems where the objective is to maximize (or minimize) some linear function (usually called the *objective function*) subject to constraints (usually expressed as linear inequalities). In regional contexts linear programming techniques have a wide sphere of application. They may be used for planning within a single region, particularly where expansion is limited by resource scarcity or capacity constraints. They are often used for urban planning, for instance in urban transportation or land use studies, where the objective may be to minimize travel costs (or other costs of movement). They may even be used for the regional aspects of national planning, where the planner's goal may be to maximize national income subject to regional equity constraints.

Despite their versatility, linear programming techniques have severe limitations for regional analysis. The assumption of linear relationships (particularly linear production functions) is at odds with the scale economies, externalities and other agglomeration factors which dominate the build-up of economic activity in certain areas. Linear programming cannot easily handle influences which are non-quantifiable, yet such forces may be important in locational contexts. They also find it difficult to accommodate household behaviour, partly because they have to rely on linear demand curves, partly because the computations usually require final product prices to be specified in advance. These objections are not insuperable, however, and provided that linear programming models can be scaled down to an operational size they have considerable scope in regional analysis.

Input–Output Analysis

A regional income model may be too highly aggregated for tracing the effects of exogenous changes on the regional economy. More precise results may be obtainable from the disaggregated input–output model. If total regional production is subdivided by industry we can derive an interindustry matrix from which the flow of goods and services can be traced from one production sector to another. However, regional input–output analysis involves a double disaggregation, since production is not only broken down by commodity but by region as well. Accordingly, such an analysis describes inter-regional trade as well as regional production.

This twofold disaggregation makes it very difficult to give regional input–output models empirical content. The data requirements are very heavy, and in particular statistics referring to inter-regional flows of goods are in most countries almost impossible to obtain except via very costly industrial survey methods. Empirical application is only a faint hope unless we make restrictive, often heroic, assumptions. These are not only the standard assumptions of all input–output models (no multiproduct industries, linear input functions, no external economies, neglect of capital formation and capacity variations) but also other assumptions required by the inter-regional framework: stable trade coefficients and fixed supply areas which in turn imply other things such as stable relative prices between regions and an absence of inter-regional competition.

For these reasons, and given the present level of information and the costs incurred in obtaining the knowledge needed for an efficient inter-regional input–output matrix, we should not be too optimistic about the fruits of inter-regional input–output research in the near future. They are important conceptually particularly for impact evaluation studies, but it is probable that little use would be made of them, at the moment, considering the rudimentary *ad hoc* character of regional planning. Moreover, the major regional problems require dynamic analysis, and it is not fully known whether the 'snapshot' static input–output model is appropriate for long-run investigations. Research is being undertaken at present[1] into the constancy of input–output coefficients, and this is a critical question for the usefulness of this technique.[2] Finally, attempts to operationalize dynamic regional input–output models are still at an experimental stage.

Technique for Area Planning (T.A.P.)

Our main reservations on the value of regional input–output models relate not to doubts about their usefulness, but to whether the cost of obtaining all the information needed can be justified. T.A.P. is a recently developed technique which still draws upon the principles of interindustry analysis, but which simplifies the input–output relations and restricts the data collection process.[3] This simplification is obtained by dividing a region's industries into major sectors and minor sectors, and recording the full interindustry transactions for the major sectors only.

Since each major sector, usually definable in terms of size

1. For example, by Professor I. G. Stewart at Edinburgh University.
2. However, regional input–output analysis does not require the assumption of strict constancy in input coefficients, only that they change in a predictable manner. For attempts to deal with variations in the coefficients see Miernyk (1968), and Miernyk and Shellhammer (1968, ch. 3).
3. See Regional Economic Development Institute of Pittsburgh *Technique for Area Planning: A Manual for the Construction and Application of a Simplified Input–Output Table* (1967) and *Development of a Manual for Economic Impact Analysis in Urban Areas* (1967).

and/or rapid growth (or decline), consists mainly of sizable firms, the necessary information is inexpensive to obtain. Interindustry transactions among the minor sectors are not estimated individually but are consolidated within the household sector account.[1] This modification means that only limited information about the minor sectors is required: information collected from the major sectors will provide details of major–minor transactions; the other data required for the minor sectors, sales to exports and purchases from imports, can be obtained from inexpensive surveys.

T.A.P. is a mongrel technique, somewhere between an input–output model and an economic base study. It avoids the costliness of the former and the undue aggregation of the latter. Although it follows base analysis in giving exports primary consideration in the final demand sector, impact estimates from T.A.P. were found to fall within 5 per cent of those resulting from comprehensive input–output studies.[2]

A T.A.P. study may be used either for projection or for evaluating the impact of alternative policies (e.g. the choice between promoting the growth of an existing firm, a new firm related to existing local activities, and a firm in an industry new to the region) on local employment or income. As with all regional planning techniques, T.A.P. is limited in what it can do and in the fields in which it may be applied. It cannot evaluate the wider effects of policies designed to achieve broader economic or non-economic objectives, but can only measure the direct effects of alternative policies on local economic activity. Moreover, T.A.P. only works effectively when applied to small, specialized areas rather than to very large, diversified regions.[3]

1. For the procedures of how this can be done see *Technique for Area Planning*, *op. cit.*, ch. 4.

2. *Technique for Area Planning*, Appendix 1.

3. For T.A.P. to be an appropriate technique a minimum value for the index of regional specialization of $\pm 0 \cdot 20$ (and a desirable value of $\pm 0 \cdot 25$) is required. This index is computed by comparing the percentage shares of total employment for each industry in the region and the nation, summing up the positive *or* negative differences between regional and national percentages, and dividing by 100.

Comparative Cost Studies

These may be employed as part of a strategy for matching industries with regions. Their objective is simply to determine, assuming established market patterns and a fixed geographical distribution of productive resources, for any given industry the region(s) in which it can achieve the lowest total costs of production and distribution to markets. The basic methodology is to obtain enough cost information to calculate total production costs incurred between and within regions. In practice, the task can be narrowed down considerably: a limited number of feasible sites can be preselected by a more general analysis; a comparative cost analysis will need only to examine those production and transport cost elements which differ significantly from one area to another. One complication, however, is that major cost differentials may arise if the optimum scale of plant in an industry varies between regions.

Comparative cost analysis is a very useful technique, but it has its limitations. It is a static analysis which would need to be repeated because of the dynamics of locational change – technological advances, changes in raw material sources or in market conditions, the development of new products. It is confined to a comparison of money cost differentials, whereas an industry may fail to take hold in a region because of attitudinal obstacles and business or worker resistance. Locational advantages and disadvantages which are not directly quantifiable can, however, be allowed for if comparative cost analysis is supplemented by scaling or latent structure techniques (Isard, 1960, ch. 7, appendix A).

A similar point is that the results of comparative cost studies, with their emphasis on direct costs, approximate to an assessment of private costs, and are therefore of more value to private firms in their location decisions than to the government with its concern with social costs and benefits. Moreover, such a study takes relative prices in a region as given, but a large industry may alter the structure of costs and prices. This leads on to the point that an effective matching study should look at the interrelationships between industries.

Industrial Complex Analysis

Emphasis on industrial interrelationships in a locational setting leads on to a consideration of industrial complex analysis (Isard, Schooler and Vietorisz, 1959). At some sacrifice in generality, the technique enables the analyst to take account of interindustry relations without having to accept the unrealistic assumptions of input–output models. At the same time, it can deal with scale economies, localization economies and price changes associated with factor substitution, which are outside the scope of input–output analysis but allowed for in comparative cost analysis.

An industrial complex may be interpreted as a set of activities occurring at a given location belonging to a group of activities that reap external economies as a result of production, marketing or other linkages. Obvious examples include a steel complex, which encompasses a chain of activities from raw materials to finished goods, or a petrochemical complex where several products are produced from a single class of raw materials.

The broad structure of an industrial complex can be determined by general knowledge of technical and/or marketing relationships. We then employ a modified input–output procedure but in the form of an interactivity not an interindustry matrix; also, we allow for non-linearities (i.e. varying input coefficients) and for alternative processes. It is also necessary to compare the costs of production at different locations, but for a set of activities not a single industry. Moreover, an industrial complex cannot be assumed to have a fixed structure regardless of location; the composition of the complex will change between regions as we allow for varying factor proportions and product mixes, scale economies and differences in the strength of urbanization and other 'spatial juxtaposition' economies.

Once again, the technique has its weaknesses. In particular, it finds difficulty in handling non-quantifiable urbanization and other location-bound external economies, and it cannot be employed in cases where interrelationships among activities are weak. On the other hand, as is suggested from its affinities with development pole theory,[1] the build-up of an industrial complex may be critical to the success of a programme to develop or regenerate a region. Also, the partial disaggregated approach that it inevitably demands may be more useful to the practical planner than macroeconomic models or general equilibrium approaches. Industrial complex analysis is a powerful tool provided it is used to complement rather than to replace other regional techniques.

Cost–Benefit Analysis

We have seen that the case for intervention via regional planning, rather than allowing market forces to allocate resources among regions, rests largely on divergences between social and private benefits and costs. This implies that government investment projects which have a regional dimension (as most do since projects have to be located somewhere!) should not be determined by narrow investment criteria but by a broader assessment of benefits relative to costs. Moreover, where public projects are location free, the choice of location should take account of regional variations in social benefits (for example, the possibility that locating a government R and D establishment in a particular previously unprogressive region may induce a higher propensity to innovate, enlarge the pool of technical and scientific personnel and give rise to other external economies there).

All this suggests that in regional planning, where public sector investment and government subsidized private invest-ment are so crucial, there should be wide scope for cost-benefit analysis. Conceptually there is, but the practical difficulties are enormous. The methodology is particularly unsatisfactory for investment projects large enough to affect relative prices and output. The answers to some problems are easy; for example, with external economies we include technological ones among the benefits but leave out pecuniary external economies which are merely transfers. But other

1. This kinship was noted above, ch. 4, p. 104.

difficulties are more intractable. What should be included in the benefits? How should benefits be evaluated in view of market imperfections, the difficulties of assigning prices to collective goods, and the 'intangible' benefits and costs which either cannot be quantified or which cannot be valued in market terms? In discounting future benefits to the present, what discount rate should be used? How should the analyst allow for uncertainty? There are no fully satisfactory answers to these questions, and the cost–benefit methodology is accordingly much less useful than appears on first sight.

On the other hand, investment decisions have to be made by governments, and a cost–benefit analysis at least forces the planner to attempt to list the costs and benefits and to quantify them. The technique is more useful for small projects, for comparing projects in the same field, and for public utility rather than social service schemes where the benefits are less easy to measure. Moreover, the objections to cost–benefit analysis in inter-regional planning are not as great as in some other spheres. There are cases where the government decides that a particular investment project is to be undertaken and then has to choose a location for it. If three or four regions were selected as feasible sites, it would be unnecessary to measure precisely all the costs and benefits since many of these would be of similar magnitude in all regions. Precise estimation is required only where regional differences in costs and benefits are believed to be large. There would then be a strong case for setting the project in the region where the present value of benefits less costs was maximized.

Systems Analysis

Some of the weaknesses of cost–benefit methodology can be avoided by the adoption of systems analysis. The advantage of systems analysis is that it does not require benefits to be incorporated into a single benefit measure but permits the use of multiple, not necessarily commensurable, measures of benefits. In activities where benefits cannot easily be measured, systems analysis helps to improve information for decisions and allows the decision-maker to see clearly the cost of achieving specified gains in each of a variety of measures related to any objective.

Whereas cost–benefit analysis was developed as a guide to government allocation in the absence of a price mechanism, systems analysis had a different origin. It was the product of years of analysis of weapons systems in the United States, a field in which the monetary quantification of benefits was in the main impossible (McKean, 1958; Quade, 1965). The core of the systems approach is an attempt to describe any problem in relation to a structure of objectives, costs and benefits. It emphasizes quantitative techniques (as in operations research), and this requires close specification of objectives in an operational manner. This presents difficulties, particularly in the public services field where objectives are often defined too widely, and where objectives have often to be framed in input terms (e.g. pupil–teacher ratios and doctor–patient ratios in the educational and health services).[1]

The aim of systems analysis is to enable the decision-maker to specify his development goals and to decide on a clear course of action more rationally.[2] This involves a systematic and quantitative investigation of objectives and a comparison of the costs, effectiveness and risks associated with alternative ways of achieving these objectives. A by-product of such an analysis is frequently additional information requirements which may aid the design of future systems.

An important aspect of systems analysis is *cost-effectiveness*, where having quantified the objectives we measure the cost and effectiveness of alternative actions to achieve them. In some cases, again government services are a primary example, the measurement of effectiveness is very imprecise, and we have to be satisfied with performance measures and standards, usually expressed via input criteria. Moreover, in regard to government policies, especially in the regional sphere, the

1. It is obvious that in these areas similar inputs can mean very different quantities and quality of services.
2. Hence, flow charts are frequently used as a first step in a systems study.

equity component is important, and although this may be incorporated in a measure of effectiveness, it may be given an independent role in the system.

Systems analysis has not been applied very much in regional and urban analysis. (However, see Hoffenberg and Devine (1966) and Teitz (1968).) Yet it is a methodology which could be used fruitfully in this field. Regional analysis is an area where a choice has often to be made among competing objectives and where any given objective may be pursued with any one of several alternative instruments. In addition, the complexities of regional problems, the relevance of non-economic (though not necessarily non-measurable) criteria and the likelihood of limited budget constraints increase the scope for systems analysis, with its methodical assessment of costs relative to outputs and of outputs relative to objectives.

Conclusion

There can be no real conclusion to this book; regional economics is changing too fast. At best, we can only offer a few indicators about its future course and direction. Some of the early work, particularly in the 1950s, fell within the scope of inter-regional macroeconomics. This branch of the subject borrowed heavily from traditional areas of economic analysis, particularly from the theory of international trade and from Keynesian macroeconomics. Although there is little doubt that more work remains to be done in this field, and it is true that regional income analysis can give rise to elegant models and intellectually fascinating problems, it would be very surprising if the future of regional economics lay in this direction. Inter-regional macroeconomics is not without policy implications – for instance, as an aid to implementing a regional stabilization policy, but there are severe limitations in the scope for a treatment of the space economy which abstracts from space itself.

The most exciting developments in the future will require explicit analysis of distance, and of the agglomeration and nodal characteristics discussed in chapters 3 and 4 of this book. The key to an improved understanding of the spatial distribution of economic activity lies in an integration of regional and urban analysis within a broader inter-regional framework. Moreover, it is not sufficient to refine the theoretical apparatus. The relationship between economic analysis and regional and urban planning will have to be investigated more deeply, and there will need to be a more willing co-operation between economists and planners. Indeed, the economist who wishes to discover how the space economy works will have to drop his disciplinary barriers and assimilate the research of the urban sociologist, economic geographer, demographer, transportation and physical planner. Although the economist has much to offer in this field, his contribution will have its maximum effect only within the broader interdisciplinary framework of 'regional science'.

References

ACKLEY, G. (1961), *Macroeconomic Theory*, Collier-Macmillan.

AIROV, J. (1963), 'The construction of interregional business cycles', *Journal of Regional Science*, vol. 5, pp. 1–20.

AIROV, J. (1967), 'Fiscal-policy theory in an inter-regional economy: general inter-regional multipliers and their application', *Papers and Proceedings of the Regional Science Association*, vol. 19, pp. 83–108.

ALONSO, W. (1964), *Location and Land Use: Towards a General Theory of Land Rent*, Harvard University Press.

• ARCHIBALD, G. C. (1967), 'Regional multiplier effects in the U.K.', *Oxford Economic Papers*, vol. 19, pp. 22–45.

BECKMANN, M. J. (1958), 'City hierarchies and the distribution of city size', *Economic Development and Cultural Change*, vol. 6, pp. 243–8.

BECKMANN, M. J. (1968), *Location Theory*, Random House.

BERRY, B. J. L. (1964), 'Cities as systems within systems of cities', *Papers and Proceedings of the Regional Science Association*, vol. 13, pp. 147–63.

BERRY, B. J. L. (1967), *Geography of Market Centres and Retail Distribution*, Prentice-Hall.

BERRY, B. J. L., and GARRISON, W. L. (1958), 'Recent development of central place theory', *Papers and Proceedings of the Regional Science Association*, vol. 4, pp. 107–121.

BIRD, P. A., and THIRLWALL, A. P. (1967), 'The incentive to invest in the new development areas', *District Bank Review*, June, no. 162, pp. 24–5.

BJORK, G. C. (1968), 'Regional adjustment to economic growth: the United States, 1880–1950', *Oxford Economic Papers*, vol. 20, pp. 81–97.

BORTS, G. H. (1960), 'The equalisation of returns and regional economic growth', *American Economic Review*, vol. 50, pp. 319–47.

BORTS, G. H. (1961), *Regional Cycles of Manufacturing Employment in the United States, 1914–53*, National Bureau of Economic Research, Princeton University Press, occasional paper, no. 73.

BORTS, G. H. (1966), 'Criteria for the evaluation of regional development programs', in Hirsch, W. Z. (ed.), *Regional Accounts for Policy Decisions*, Johns Hopkins Press, pp. 183–218.

BORTS, G. H., and STEIN, J. L. (1964), *Economic Growth in a Free Market*, Columbia University Press.

Bos, H. C. (1965), *Spatial Dispersion of Economic Activity*, North-Holland.

BOUDEVILLE, J. R. (1966), *Problems of Regional Economic Planning*, Edinburgh University Press.

BRAZER, H. E. (1959), *City Expenditures in the United States*, National Bureau of Economic Research, Princeton University Press, occasional paper, no. 66.

BROWN, A. J., *et al.* (1967), 'The "Green Paper" on the development areas', *Economic Review*, Appendix, no. 40, May, p. 33.

BROWN, A. J., *et al.* (1968), 'Regional problems and regional policy', *Economic Review*, no. 46, November, pp. 42–51.

CAMERON, G. C., and REID, G. L. (1966), *Scottish Economic Planning and the Attraction of Industry*, University of Glasgow Social and Economic Studies, occasional paper, no. 6.

CAO-PINNA, V. (1961), 'Problems of establishing and using regional input-output accounting', in Isard, W., and Cumberland, J. H. (eds.), *Regional Economic Planning: Techniques of Analysis for Less Developed Areas*, Organisation for European Co-operation and Development, pp. 305–38.

CARROLL, J. D., and BEVIS, H. W. (1957), 'Predicting local travel in urban regions', *Papers and Proceedings of the Regional Science Association*, vol. 3, pp. 183–97.

CARRUTHERS, W. I. (1967), 'Major shopping centres in England and Wales, 1961', *Regional Studies*, vol. 1, pp. 65–81.

CHAPIN, F. S., JR (1965), *Urban Land Use Planning*, Illinois University Press.

CHINITZ, B. (1961), 'Contrasts in agglomeration: New York and Pittsburgh', *American Economic Review*, Papers, vol. 51, pp. 279–89.

CHIPMAN, J. S. (1950), *The Theory of Inter-Sectoral Money Flows and Income Formation*, Johns Hopkins Press.

CHRISTALLER, W. (1966), *Central Places in Southern Germany*, translated by Baskin, C. W., Prentice-Hall.

CLARK, C. (1966), 'Industrial location and economic potential', *Lloyds Bank Review*, October, no. 82, pp. 1–17.

CLARK, C., and PETERS, G. H. (1964), 'Steering employment by taxes and rebates', *Town and Country Planning*, vol. 32, March, pp. 145–9.

COLENUTT, R. J. (1968), 'Building linear predictive models for urban planning', *Regional Studies*, vol. 2.

DACEY, M. F. (1966), 'Population of places in a central place hierarchy', *Journal of Regional Science*, vol. 6, pp. 27–33.

DE SCITOVSKY, T. (1958), *Economic Theory and Western European Integration*, Allen and Unwin.

DEVLETOGLOU, N. E. (1965), 'A dissenting view of duopoly and spatial competition', *Economica*, vol. 32, pp. 140–60.

DOMAR, E. D. (1957), *Essays in the Theory of Economic Growth*, Oxford University Press.

DOWIE, R. (1968), 'Government assistance to industry: a review of the legislation of the 1960s', *Ashford Study Paper 2*, University of Kent Centre for Research in the Social Sciences.

DUNN, E. S. (1956), 'The market potential concept and the analysis of location', *Papers and Proceedings of the Regional Science Association*, vol. 2, pp. 183–94.

EASTERLIN, R. A. (1958), 'Long term regional income changes: some suggested factors', *Papers and Proceedings of the Regional Science Association*, vol. 2, pp. 313–25.

EASTERLIN, R. A. (1960), 'Regional growth in income: long term tendencies', in Kuznets, S., Miller, A. R., and Easterlin, R. A., *Population Redistribution and Economic Growth, United States, 1870–1950*, vol. 2, American Philosophical Society, pp. 141–203.

ENGERMAN, S. (1965), 'Regional aspects of stabilisation policy', in Musgrave, R. A. (ed.), *Essays in Fiscal Federalism*, Brookings Institution, pp. 7–62.

FERGUSON, C. E. (1966), *Microeconomic Theory*, Irwin.

FRIEDRICH, C. J. (1929), *Alfred Weber's Theory of the Location of Industries*, Chicago University Press.

GARBARINO, J. W. (1954), 'Some implications of regional and industrial differences in unemployment', *Proceedings of the Western Economic Association*, paper read at conference.

GIBBS, J. P. (1961), *Urban Research Methods*, Van Nostrand.

GREEN, F. H. W. (1950), 'Urban hinterlands in England and Wales: an analysis of bus services', *Geographical Journal*, vol. 116, pp. 64–88, and vol. 132 (1966), pp. 263–6.

GREENHUT, M. L. (1956), *Plant Location in Theory and Practice*, North Carolina University Press.

GUPTA, S. P., and HUTTON, J. P. (1968), 'Economies of scale in local government services', *Royal Commission on Local Government in England*, Research Studies, no. 3, p. 44.

HAMMER, C., and IKLÉ, F. C. (1957), 'Intercity telephone and airline traffic related to distance and the "propensity to interact"', *Sociometry*, vol. 20, pp. 306–16.

HANNA, F. A. (1957), 'Analysis of interstate income differentials: theory and practice', National Bureau of Economic Research Studies in Income and Wealth, vol. 21, *Regional Income*, Princeton University Press, pp. 113–61.

HANNA, F. A. (1959), *State Income Differentials, 1919–54*, Duke University Press.

HANSEN, N. M. (1967), 'Development pole theory in a regional context', *Kyklos*, vol. 20, pp. 709–25.

HARRIS, C. D. (1954), 'The market as a factor in the localisation of industry in the United States', *Annals of the Association of American Geographers*, vol. 44, pp. 315–48.

HARROD, R. F. (1948), *Towards a Dynamic Economics*, Macmillan.

HARTMAN, L. M., and SECKLER, D. (1967), 'Toward the application of dynamic growth theory to regions', *Journal of Regional Science*, vol. 7, pp. 166–73.

HEATHFIELD, D., and HILTON, K. (1968), 'A surrogate for regional estimates of capital stock: a comment', *Oxford University Bulletin of the Institute of Economics and Statistics*, vol. 30, pp. 263–6.

HEMMING, M. F. W. (1963), 'The regional problem', *Economic Review*, no. 25, pp. 40–57.

HIRSCH, W. Z. (1959), 'Expenditure implications of metropolitan growth and consolidation', *Review of Economics and Statistics*, vol. 41, pp. 232–41.

HOFFENBERG, M., and DEVINE, E. J. (1966), 'Influence of national decisions on regional economies', in Hirsch, W. Z. (ed.), *Regional Accounts for Policy Decisions*, Johns Hopkins Press, pp. 156–75.

HOOVER, E. M. (1948), *The Location of Economic Activity*, McGraw-Hill.

HOTELLING, H. (1929), 'Stability in competition', *Economic Journal*, vol. 39, pp. 41–57.

HOWARD, R. S. (1968), *The Movement of Manufacturing Industry in the United Kingdom, 1945–65*, Board of Trade.

HUGHES, J. T., and KOZLOWSKI, J. (1968), 'Threshold analysis – an economic tool for town and regional planning', *Urban Studies*, vol. 5, pp. 132–43.

HUTTON, J. P., and HARTLEY, K. (1968), 'A regional payroll tax', *Oxford Economic Papers*, vol. 20, pp. 417–26.

ISARD, W. (1956), *Location and Space-Economy*, M.I.T. Press.

ISARD, W. (1960), *Methods of Regional Analysis*, ch. 7, Appendix A, M.I.T. Press, pp. 281–93.

ISARD, W. (1965), 'Spatial organization and regional planning: some hypotheses for econometric analysis', in *Pontificiae Academiae Scientiarum, Scripta Varia*, no. 28, *An Econometric Approach to Development Planning*, North-Holland, pp. 1003–28.

ISARD, W., and CUMBERLAND, J. H. (1961), *Regional Economic Planning: Techniques of Analysis for Less-Developed Areas*, Organisation for European Co-operation and Development.

ISARD, W., SCHOOLER, E. W., and VIETORISZ, T. (1959), *Industrial Complex Analysis and Regional Development*, M.I.T. Press.

ISARD, W., and SMITH, T. E. (1967), 'Location games: with applications to classic location problems', *Papers and Proceedings of the Regional Science Association*, vol. 19, pp. 45–80.

JAMES, B. G. S. (1964), 'The incompatibility of industrial and trading cultures: a critical appraisal of the growth point concept', *Journal of Industrial Economics*, vol. 13, pp. 90–94.

KLAASSEN, L. H. (1965), *Area Economic and Social Redevelopment: Guidelines for Programmes*, Organisation for European Co-operation and Development.

KOZLOWSKI, J., and HUGHES, J. T. (1967), 'Urban threshold theory and analysis', *Journal of the Town Planning Institute*, vol. 53, pp. 55–60.

KOZLOWSKI, J., and HUGHES, J. T. (1968), 'Threshold analysis – an economic tool for town and regional planning', *Urban Studies*, vol. 5, pp. 132–43.

LAKSHMANAN, T. R., and HANSEN, W. G. (1965), 'A retail market potential model', *Journal of American Institute of Planners*, vol. 31, pp. 134–43.

LASUEN, J. R. (1969), 'On growth poles', *Urban Studies*, vol. 6, pp. 137-61.

LEFEBER, L. (1958), *Allocation in Space*, North-Holland.

LEFEBER, L. (1966), *Location and Regional Planning*, Centre for Planning and Economic Research, Athens.

LEONTIEF, W., and STROUT, A. A. (1963), 'Multiregional input–output analysis', in Barna, T. (ed.), *Structural Interdependence and Economic Development*, Macmillan, pp. 119–50.

LERNER, A. P., and SINGER, H. W. (1939), 'Some notes on duopoly and spatial competition', *Journal of Political Economy*, vol. 45, pp. 145–86.

LEVEN, C. (1964), 'Establishing goals for regional economic development', *Journal of the American Institute of Planners*, vol. 30, pp. 100–110.

LEWIS, J. P., and TRAILL, A. L. (1968), 'The assessment of shopping potential and the demand for shops', *Town Planning Review*, vol. 38, pp. 317–26.

LOASBY, B. J. (1965), 'Location of industry: thirty years of "planning"', *District Bank Review*, no. 156, pp. 29–52.

LOASBY, B. J. (1967), 'Making location policy work', *Lloyds Bank Review*, no. 83, pp. 34–47.

LÖSCH, A. (1954), *The Economics of Location*, Yale University Press.

LUTTRELL, W. F. (1962), *Factory Location and Industrial Movement* (2 vols.), National Institute of Economic and Social Research.

MACHLUP, F. (1943), *International Trade and the National Income Multiplier*, Blakiston.

MACKAY, D. I. (1968), 'Industrial structure and regional growth: a methodological problem', *Scottish Journal of Political Economy*, vol. 15, pp. 129–43.

MALISZ, B. (1969), 'Implications of threshold theory for urban and regional planning', *Journal of the Town Planning Institute*, vol. 55, pp. 108–10.

MATILLA, J. M., and THOMPSON, W. R. (1955), 'The measurement of the economic base of the metropolitan area', *Land Economics*, vol. 31, pp. 214–28.

MCCRONE, G. (1968), 'The application of regional accounting in the United Kingdom', *Regional Studies*, vol. 1, pp. 39–45.

MCCRONE, G. (1969), *Regional Policy in Britain*, Allen and Unwin.

MCKEAN, R. N. (1958), *Efficiency in Government through Systems Analysis*, Wiley.

MEADE, J. E. (1961), *A Neo-Classical Theory of Economic Growth*, Allen and Unwin.

MERA, K. (1967), 'Tradeoff between aggregate efficiency and inter-regional equity: a static analysis', *Quarterly Journal of Economics*, vol. 81, pp. 658–74.

MIERNYK, W. H. (1966), 'Experience under the British Local Employment Acts of 1960 and 1963', *Industrial and Labor Relations Review*, vol. 20, pp. 30–49.

MIERNYK, W. H. (1968), 'Long-range forecasting with a regional input–output model', *Western Economic Journal*, vol. 6, pp. 165–76.

MIERNYK, W. H., and SHELLHAMMER, K. L. (1968), *Simulating Regional Economic Development with an Input–Output Model*, Regional Research Institute, West Virginia.

MILLS, E. S., and LAV, M. R. (1964), 'A model of market areas with free entry', *Journal of Political Economy*, vol. 72, pp. 278–88.

MYRDAL, G. (1957), *Economic Theory and Underdeveloped Regions*, Duckworth.

NEEDLEMAN, L., and SCOTT, B. (1964), 'Regional problems and location of industry policy in Britain', *Urban Studies*, vol. 1, pp. 153–73.

NEFF, P. (1959), 'Interregional cyclical differentials', *American Economic Review*, Papers, vol. 39, pp. 105–19.

NICHOLSON, R. J. (1956), 'The regional location of industry', *Economic Journal*, vol. 66, pp. 467–81.

NORTH, D. C. (1955), 'Location theory and regional economic growth', *Journal of Political Economy*, vol. 63, pp. 243–58.

NYSTUEN, J. D., and DACEY, M. F. (1961), 'A graph theory interpretation of nodal regions', *Papers and Proceedings of the Regional Science Association*, vol. 7, pp. 29–42.

OKUN, B., and RICHARDSON, R. W. (1961), 'Regional income inequality and internal population migration', *Economic Development and Cultural Change*, vol. 9, pp. 128–43.

PEACOCK, A. T. (1965), 'Towards a theory of inter-regional fiscal policy', *Public Finance*, vol. 20, pp. 7–17.

PERLOFF, H. S., DUNN, E. S., JR, LAMPARD, E. E., and MUTH, R. F. (1960), *Regions, Resources and Economic Growth*, Johns Hopkins Press.

PERROUX, F. (1955), 'Note sur la notion de pôle de croissance', *Économie Appliquée*, vol. 7, pp. 307–20.

PERROUX, F. (1964), *L'économie du XXe siècle*, part 2, Presses Universitaires de France.

PFOUTS, R. W. (1960), *The Techniques of Urban Economic Analysis*, Chandler-Davis.

PRATT, R. T. (1968), 'An appraisal of the minimum requirements technique', *Economic Geography*, vol. 44, pp. 117–24.

PREST, A. R. (1968), *The U.K. Economy: A Manual of Applied Economics*, 2nd edn, Weidenfeld and Nicolson.

QUADE, E. S. (1965), *Analysis for Military Decisions*, Rand Corporation.

RICHARDSON, H. W. (1969), *Regional Economics: Location Theory, Urban Structure and Regional Change*, Weidenfeld and Nicolson.

ROMANS, J. T. (1965), *Capital Exports and Growth among U.S. Regions*, Wesleyan University Press.

SARGENT, J. R. (1968), 'Regional economic planning', in Prest, A. R. (ed.), *Public Sector Economics*, Manchester University Press, pp. 191–200.

SCHWARTZ, C. F., and GRAHAM, R. E., JR (1956), *Personal Income by States since 1929*, U.S. Government Printing Office.

SINGER, H. W. (1936), 'The "courbe des populations": a parallel to Pareto's law', *Economic Journal*, vol. 46, pp. 254–63.

SJAASTAD, L. A. (1962), 'The costs and returns of human migration', *Journal of Political Economy*, supplement, vol. 70, pp. 80–93.

SMAILES, A. E. (1944), 'The urban hierarchy in England and Wales', *Geography*, vol. 29, pp. 41–51.

SMITH, R. D. P. (1968), 'The changing urban hierarchy', *Regional Studies*, vol. 2, pp. 1–19.

SMOLENSKY, E. (1961), 'Industrialisation and income inequality: recent United States experience', *Papers and Proceedings of the Regional Science Association*, vol. 7, pp. 67–88.

STEELE, D. B. (1969), 'Regional multipliers in Great Britain', *Oxford Economic Papers*, vol. 21, pp. 268–92.

STEVENS, B. (1961), 'An application of game theory to problems in location strategy', *Papers and Proceedings of the Regional Science Association*, vol. 7, pp. 143–58.

STILWELL, F. J. B. (1969), 'Regional growth and structural adaption', *Urban Studies*, vol. 6, pp. 162-78.

STOUFFER, S. A. (1940), 'Intervening opportunities: a theory relating mobility and distance', *American Sociological Review*, vol. 5, pp. 845–67.

TAYLOR, J. (1967), 'A surrogate for regional estimates of capital stock', *Oxford University Bulletin of the Institute of Economics and Statistics*, vol. 29, pp. 289–99.

TEITZ, M. B. (1968), 'Cost effectiveness: a systems approach to analysis of urban services', *Journal of American Institute of Planners*, vol. 34, pp. 303–11.

THIRLWALL, A. P. (1966), 'The Local Employment Acts 1960 and 1963: a progress report', *Yorkshire Bulletin of Economic and Social Research*, vol. 18, pp. 49–63.

THOMAS, M. D. (1964), 'The export base and development stages theories of regional economic growth: an appraisal', *Land Economics*, vol. 11, pp. 421–32.

TIEBOUT, C. M. (1956), 'Exports and regional economic growth', *Journal of Political Economy*, vol. 64. Also 'Reply' by North, D. C. and 'Rejoinder' by Tiebout, C. M., pp. 160–69.

TIEBOUT, C. M. (1960), 'The community income multiplier: a case study', in Pfouts, R. W. (ed.), *The Techniques of Urban Economic Analysis*, Chandler-Davis.

TIEBOUT, C. W. (1962), *The Community Economic Base Study*, Committee for Economic Development.

TINBERGEN, J. (1952), *On the Theory of Economic Policy*, North-Holland.

TINBERGEN, J. (1954), *Centralisation and Decentralisation in Economic Policy*, North-Holland.

TINBERGEN, J. (1961), 'The spatial dispersion of production: a hypothesis', *Schweizerishe Zeitschrift für Volkwirtschaft und Statistik*, vol. 97, pp. 412–19.

TINBERGEN, J. (1965), 'The economic framework of regional planning', *The Econometric Approach to Development Planning*, North-Holland, pp. 1233–44.

ULLMAN, E., and DACEY, M. F. (1960), 'The minimum requirements approach to the urban economic base', *Papers and Proceedings of the Regional Science Association*, vol. 6, pp. 175–94.

VINING, R. (1948), 'The region as a concept in business cycle analysis', *Econometrica*, vol. 16, pp. 201–18.

WEISS, S. J., and GOODING, E. C. (1968), 'Estimation of differential multipliers in a small regional economy', *Land Economics*, vol. 44, pp. 235–44.

WILLIAMSON, J. G. (1965), 'Regional inequality and the process of national development', *Economic Development and Cultural Change*, vol. 13, pp. 3–45.

WILSON, A. J. (1967), 'Towards comprehensive planning models', paper presented to the Conference of the Regional Science Association, London, August 1967 (mimeo).

WILSON, A. J. (1968), 'Inter-regional commodity flows: entropy maximizing approaches', Centre for Environmental Studies, working paper, no. 19.

WILSON, T. (1967), 'Finance for regional industrial development', *Three Banks Review*, no. 75, pp. 3–23.

WILSON, T. (1968), 'The regional multiplier – a critique', *Oxford Economic Papers*, vol. 20, pp. 374–93.

ZIPF, G. K. (1946), 'The P_1P_2/D hypothesis on the intercity movement of persons', *American Sociological Review*, vol. 11, pp. 677–86.

Index

Accounts, regional 139–41
Ackley, G. 47
Ad hoc methods of estimating base activity 28–9
Adjustment mechanism in balance of payments 24–6
Agglomeration
  in the city 86–7
  economies 100, 102, 106, 118, 126, 132
  function 74–5
  and growth regions 57
  and location 69, 70–73, 78, 81
  in space 67, 69
  in Weberian theory 73–7
Airov, J. 22, 38, 40
Alonso, W. 85
Archibald, G.C. 34, 35, 36

Balance-of-payments problems of regions 24–6
Barlow Commission 129
Beckmann, M.J. 92
Berry, B.J.L. 88, 94
Bevis, H.W. 100
Bid rent functions 85–6
Bird, P.A. 128
Bjork, G.G. 59
Board of Trade 130, 131
Borts, G.H. 37, 46, 50, 59, 128
Bos, H.C. 70, 93
Boudeville, J.R. 68, 104, 119
Boundary conditions 111, 116
Brazer, H.E. 90
Brown, A.J. 34, 63, 129, 137
Business cycles 37–40

multiplier-accelerator model of 40–44
  time path of 43–4

Cable, J.R. 131
Cameron, G.C. 84
Cao-Pinna, V. 141
Capital flows
  and balance of payments 26
  and regional growth 49, 50, 52–3, 54–5, 58, 62–3, 65
Carroll, J.D. 100
Carruthers, W.I. 94
Central Borders Plan 138
Central place theory 88–91
  criticisms of 91
  and growth points 103–4, 106
  and rank–size rule 91–4
Chapin, F.S. 139
Chicago 33
Chinitz, B. 72
Chipman, J.S. 23
Christaller, W. 88
Clark, C. 121
Colenutt, R.J. 117
Community income multiplier 33
Comparative cost analysis 83, 145
Complementary region 88
Conditions of stability in regional income model 22–3
Convergence of incomes
  empirical evidence on 58–62
  influences on 55–8
  in United Kingdom 60–62
  in United States 59–60

Cost
  of congestion 72, 83, 84, 100,
    105, 123, 126, 133
  differentials between sites 79,
    145
  marginal 79, 117–18, 123
  opportunity 126, 127
  social, of migration 123
  of urban development 124, 138
Cost–benefit analysis 147–8, 149
Cost–effectiveness 149
Cumberland, J.H. 139
Cyclical sensitivity and regional
    trade 38–40

Dacey, M.F. 30, 68, 88, 92
Data
  collection 109, 143
  limitations 62, 116, 140, 142
Decentralization in planning 110
Decision criteria and location
    80–84
Development areas 128, 129, 130,
    131
Devine, E.J. 150
Devletoglou, N.E. 78
Differential multiplier 32–3
Differential shifts 46, 126
Distance
  between urban centres 96–7
  variables in gravity model 99–
    100, 101, 102
Distribution of Industry Act (1945)
    129
Domar, E.S. 47
Dowie, R. 128
Dunn, E.S., Jr 46, 53, 101, 126
Duopoly 78

Easterlin, R.A. 59
East Midlands 101–2, 135
Economies of scale 71, 72, 76,
    100, 104, 105, 126, 146
  in urban government services
    90
Economists, attitude to regional
    problems 13–14

Efficiency and equity in planning
    117, 118–19
Elasticity of demand 79
Employment
  growth in 63, 64, 65
  as proxy for income 27
Endogenous-lagged variables 113
Engerman, S. 22, 23
Export base theory 19–20, 144
  applications of 27–31
  and cycles 37
  empirical test of 31–2
  and growth 53–5
  and size of region 20
External economies 57, 71, 72–3,
    76–7, 81, 86–7, 100, 104, 126,
    132, 141, 146, 147

Factor flows
  and balance of payments 25–6
  and regional growth 49–50,
    52–3, 54–5, 62–4, 65
Ferguson, C.E. 78
Fixed or flexible targets 111, 115
'Footloose' industry 80, 125
Friedrich, C.J. 73
Full employment and regional
    problems 14, 50
Future development of regional
    economics 151–2

Game theory in location 76–7
Garbarino, J.W. 37
Garrison, W.L. 88
Gibbs, J.P. 139
Goal conflicts 112, 117–19, 150
Goals of policy 120
Gooding, E.C. 32
Government sector in regional
    income model 21, 22–3
Graham, R.E. 59
Graph analysis 68
Gravity models 97–102
Green, F.H.W. 94
Greenhut, M.L. 70, 79, 84
'Grey' areas 129, 137

Growth
  alternative approaches to regional 45–6
  Harrod–Domar model of 47–50
  and industrial structure 46–7
  in nation and region compared 45
  neo-classical 50–53
  testing of models 62–5
Growth points 102–7, 128
  and regional planning 136–8
Growth pole 72, 104, 147
Gupta, S.P. 90

Hammer, C. 98, 100
Hanna F.A. 59, 60
Hansen, N.M. 104, 107
Hansen, W.G. 98
Harris, C.D. 101
Harrod, R.F. 47
Harrod–Domar model and regions 47–50
Hartley, K. 121
Hartman, L.M. 54
Hatvany, D. 32
Heathfield, D. 63
Hemming, M.F.W. 46, 128
Hierarchical marginal service 89
Hilton, K. 63
Hirsch, W.Z. 90
Hirschman, A.O. 72
Hoffenberg, M. 150
Homogeneous regions 17–18
Hoover, E.M. 70, 72, 73
Hotelling, H. 78
Howard, R.S. 130
Hughes, J.T. 124, 138
Hunt Committee 129, 137
Hutton, J.P. 90, 121

Iklé, F.C. 98, 100
Impact evaluation studies 140, 143, 144
Imports and the multiplier 23, 34, 36, 39
Income

convergence of 55–8
evidence on 58–62
inter-regional, model 20–27
levels in U.K. 65
property 58, 59
spillovers 23–4
Index of surplus workers 29
Industrial complex analysis 104, 146–7
Industrial development certificates 130–31
Industrial structure
  and cycles 37
  and growth 46–7
  and policy 126
Inertia in location 81, 83
Inflation and migration 123–4
Input–output access 46, 57
Input–output analysis 141, 142–3, 144, 146
Instrumental variables 114
Instruments of regional policy 127–8, 129–30
Interdependence in location 78–80
Interest rate as an equilibrating mechanism 51
Investment 34–5, 41
  regional shares in 62–3
Isard, W. 70, 71, 72, 76, 77, 100, 104, 110, 139, 145, 146
Isodapanes 73–5

James, B.G.S. 107

Klaassen, L.H. 117
Kozlowski, J. 124, 138

Lakshmanan, T.R. 98
Lampard, E.E. 46, 53, 126
Lasuen, J.R. 104
Lav, M.R. 89
Lefeber, L. 70, 117
Leontief, W.W. 101
Lerner, A.P. 78
Leven, C. 115
Lewis, J.P. 98

Linear programming 141–2
Loasby, B.J. 84, 128
Local Employment Act (1960) 129
Local value added 35
Localization economies 71, 73, 76
Location
  and agglomeration economies 70–73
  basis for, decisions 80–84
  in cities 84–7
  and gravity models 101
  of industry policy, case for and against 125–8
    in Britain 128–32
  interdependence of 78–80
  and transport costs 77–8
  Weber's theory of 73–7
Location quotients 29–30, 31, 32, 36
Locational weight 73, 74
Lösch, A. 70, 78, 88
Luttrell, W.F. 80, 84

Machlup, F. 38
Mackay, D.I. 46
Macroeconomics in regional analysis 17–18, 19–65 *passim*, 151
Malisz, B. 124
Marginal cost
  curve 79
  pricing rules 117–18
  social, of migration 123
Marginal propensity to consume, role of 22–3, 24, 38
Market forces 14, 55–8, 121–2
Market orientation 69, 80, 81, 82
Market potential analysis 101
Mattila, J.M. 29
Maturity characteristics 55–6
McCrone, G. 128, 139
McKean, R.N. 149
Meade, J.E. 51
Mera, K. 118
Miernyk, W.H. 128, 143

Migration
  and balance of payments 26
  effects of 56, 122–3, 124
  and inflation 123–4
  subsidies 122–5
  in U.K. 65
Mills, E.S. 89
Minimum requirements technique 30–31
Minimum transport cost site 73–6
Multilevel fiscal system 90
Multiplier
  accelerator model 40–44
  base 6
  community income 33
  differential 32–3
  estimation of 31–6
  restrictive assumptions of 33
Muth, R.F. 46, 53, 126
Myrdal, G. 62

Needleman, L. 128
Neff, P. 37
Neo-classical
  growth models 50–53
  implications for regional economics 13, 14
Nicholson, R.J. 80
Nodal regions 67–9, 109
Nodes in space 88–107 *passim*
North, D.C. 53
North-East Scotland, base service ratio in 31–2
Northern Economic Planning Council 135
Nystuen, J.D. 68

Objective function 141
Okun, B. 122
Oligopoly and external economies 72–3

Peacock, A.T. 22
Peck, M.J. 100
Perfect competition 50, 117
Perloff, H.S. 46, 53, 59, 126
Perroux, F. 72, 104

Personal contacts 80
Peters, G.H. 121
Pfouts, R.W. 27
Planning
  and economics 133–4, 151–2
  of growth points 105
  models 113–15
    and predictive models 111–13
    solution to 115
  physical 133–4
  region 109–10
  regional and national 116–17
  techniques 139–50
  urban 133, 141
Polarization flows 67–8, 103, 105
Policy
  alternatives 120–28 *passim*
  in Britain 128–32
  case for location of industry
    125–7
  effects of 130–31
  instruments 127–8, 129–30
  money costs of 131
  reasons for development of
    14–15
Population
  and agglomeration 80
  overspill 137
  potential 100
  projections 136
Portsmouth, New Hampshire 32
Potential 98, 100
Pratt, R.T. 30
Prest, A.R. 131
Price mechanism 117–18, 121,
  142, 145, 147
Pricing systems 80
Profit maximization and location
  81–2
Proportional shifts 46, 126
Propulsive industries 104, 106
Psychic income 81, 84, 125
Pullen, M.J. 101

Quade, E.S.1 49

Range of a good 88, 89

Rank-size rule 91–4, 96
Regional balance 125
Regional Economic Planning
  Boards 132
  Councils 132–8 *passim*
  reports of 134–8
Regional employment premium
  128, 130
Registrar General's population
  forecasts 136
Reid, G.L. 84
Reilly, W.J. 100
Rent in urban locations 84–6
Repercussion waves 38
Resource allocation within regions
  54–5
Retail trade forecasts via gravity
  models 98–9, 101–2
Revenue maximization 82–3
Richardson, H.W. 70
Richardson, R.W. 122
Romans, J.T. 50, 59

St Boswells 138
Samuelson, P.A. 43
Sargent, J.R. 101, 133
Satisficing behaviour 84
Scaling and latent structure tech-
  niques 145
Schooler, E.W. 71, 104, 146
Schwartz, C.F. 59
Scitovsky, T. de 26
Scott, B. 128
Seckler, D. 54
Shellhammer, K.L. 143
Singer, H.W. 78, 91, 94
Size variable in gravity models
  99–100, 101
Sjaastad, L.A. 122
Smailes, A.E. 94
Smith, R.D.P. 94
Smith, T.E. 76, 77
Smolensky, E. 59
South-East Study 137
Spacelessness assumption 17
Spatial competition

Stabilization policy 22–3
Steele, D.B. 36
Stein, J.L. 46, 50, 59
Stevens, B. 77
Stewart, I.G. 143
Stewart, J.Q. 99
Stilwell, F.J.B. 46
Strout, A.A. 101
Subsidies
  to migrants 122–5
  wage, capital and price compared 128
Supermultiplier 35
Survey methods 27–8
Systems analysis 148–50

Target
  variables 113–14
  fixed v. flexible 11, 115
Taylor, J. 63
Technique for area planning 143–4
Technological change 14
  and agglomeration 56–7, 147
Teitz, M.B. 150
Thirlwall, A.P. 128
Thomas, M.D. 53
Thompson, W.R. 29
Threshold of demand 88, 89
Time path of cycles 43–4
Tinbergen, J. 93, 115
Town and Country Planning Act (1947) 129
Trade, inter-regional
  and cycles 37, 39–40, 41, 42
  and gravity model 101
Traill, A.L. 98

Transitivity 68
Transport costs and location 77–8, 79

Ullman, E. 30
Uncertainty and location 79, 81
United Kingdom
  changing urban hierarchy in 94–7
  income estimates in 61
  location of industry policy in 128–32
  regional growth in 64–5
United States
  rank–size rule in 94
  regional income differentials in 59–60
Urban centres and location 84–7
Urban hierarchy 69, 88, 91–3 *passim*
  changes in 94–7
  and regional development 96
Urbanization economies 72

Vietorisz, T. 71, 104, 146
Vining, R. 38, 40

Weber, A. 71, 73, 77
Weiss, S.J. 32
Williamson, J.G. 59
Wilson, A.J. 98, 101
Wilson, T. 35, 128
Winnetka 33

Zipf, G.K. 91, 98
Zone of influence 67–8, 103, 105, 106, 107